UNDERSTANDING STRESS
A Multidimensional Approach

Sumitra Srivastava
Consultant Psychologist

Regency Publications
New Delhi

ISBN 81-86030-63-8

Published by Regency Publications, 20/36–G, Old Market, West Patel Nagar, New Delhi 110 008, and printed at Radiant Printers, New Delhi 110 008, Phones: 571 2539, 574 0038; Telefax: 578 3571.

ACKNOWLEDGEMENTS

I begin with my family. My husband Dr. R.C. Srivastava, son Rajat and daughter Ruchira helped me throughout the writing of this book with their constructive criticisms, challenges, support and assistance in all possible ways in the preparation of the manuscript.

Dr. K.D. Broota, Professor of Psychology at the University of Delhi had in fact suggested to me to write a comprehensive non-technical book on stress. The present book is in response to his suggestion.

Artist Shri Satish Chauhan, an upcoming student architect Gaurav Mathur and the noted Cartoonist Priyaraj prepared several illustrations incorporated in the book.

Dr. Nagarathanam of the Vivekanand Kendra, Bangalore helped me in clarifying the role of Yogic practices in stress reduction and permitted me to reproduce the three forms of Shavasana used at the Vivekananda Kendra.

Experts in the field like Hans Selye, Richard Lazarus, Mariam Frankenhaeuscr and Aaron Antonovsky whose researches and insights in stress phenomenon helped me to develop my conceptions about thc stress phenomenon.

Shri Tika Ram who readily and willingly typed out a part of the manuscript.

To all these people, I am extremely indebted and express my sincere appreciation and thanks to all of them.

I am also grateful to Shri A.K. Verma of the Regency Publications for undertaking the publication of the book and bringing it out in such a short time and in such a fine form.

New Delhi
June, 1998

Sumitra Srivastava

PREFACE

Scientific study of stress as an integral part of psycho-biological sciences owes its origin to Hans Selye who started his pioneering work during the third decade of the twentieth century. His researches are based on the works of Claude Bernard and Walter Cannon. While Bernard had demonstrated the value of stability of internal environment and insisted on its maintenance at all costs, Walter Cannon added to it the concept of fight-flight as an essential mechanism for survival. This response and its regulation being the core of stress-response form the focus of the book.

This book is written on the premise that stress is an essential part of the process of living. The understanding of this phenomenon must help the reader to utilise the theoretical knowledge to cope with problems of life in its various spheres. The book is not addressed to any particular group of readers since the basic concepts about stress and its management remain the same in every field.

Spread over 11 chapters, the book covers both the theoretical and practical aspects in dealing with the problems of stress.

Chapters 1 to 5 deal with the basic theoretical aspect of stress and the latter chapters are concerned with the applied aspects. Chapter 6 deals with the effect of stress on health specially when it is not coped with effectively. Chapter 7 provides an overview of the techniques currently being utilised to measure stress. No claim is made to assert that the contents of this chapter are exhaustive. At the same time it is enough to help a reader think out a strategy to measure stress in a research study or in a practical field. The chapter on social support deals with one variable that is considered to be the single most important variable in preventing, containing and overcoming stress. There are two chapters on stress management that deal with self-help and helping others to overcome or prevent stress. The chapter on 'Indian View of Stress and Coping' is an attempt at presenting the traditional ideas in the ideology that control the thought and behaviour of the people in India. This should help in understanding, in their cultural context, various behaviour forms, that otherwise appear to be incoherent or irrelevant, are actually an attempt at coping with stress.

Throughout the book, care has been taken to avoid a populist approach as well as complex scientific theorisation. This middle of the road approach should have an appeal to both the curious and the serious minded reader.

June, 1998
New Delhi

Sumitra Srivastava

CONTENTS

CHAPTER 1

INTRODUCTION

The problem of stress is as old as life. At no time in the history of humankind was life a smooth sailing predictable routine. There is nothing to vouchsafe that our stone-age ancestors lived an easy life. Hunting for food and clothing, looking for shelter and protecting oneself from wild and deadly animals was not an easy job. In comparison our lives today are much more comfortable and secure. Most of our problems are being taken care of by society and for many others there are new scientific inventions every day.

But for this man has paid a heavy price and this is reflected practically in every aspect of his life. Cities have become the centre of all activities. Thousands of people migrate to the cities in the hope of a better life, but they end up living a life of privation — often living on pavements. Uprooted from their own homes they struggle in search of an identity. They also feel a pressing need to justify their migration and for this they soon fall in the rat race to work more, to earn more and to spend more. This leaves them hardly any time or energy for relaxation or recreation. People often start avoiding social interaction, for socialization means time. All this takes a heavy toll in terms of health and efficiency. A recent Report of ILO has expressed serious concern about the problem of mounting cost of production that the industrialized nations are facing due to the payment of heavy medical and insurance bills for their workers. This, is in addition to the decreasing efficiency, lost man days and increased accident rates. Medical scientists are perturbed that all their efforts to control the killer diseases like plague, smallpox and tuberculosis have been negated by an increase in the non-infectious diseases like gastric ulcers, cancers of various types and the cardio-vascular diseases. The current increase in the problems of delinquency, truancy, prostitution and addictions of various forms are causing concern to social scientists. On the social front the scene is not very bright. A constant struggle with problems make people short-tempered and insensitive to others' needs and feelings. Social withdrawal is a common pattern of behaviour adding to their hassles, since whatever help or support they would have obtained is lost because of their unsocial behaviour. Increase in depression and psychiatric help sought gives enough evidence of the sorry state of affairs created by the cumulative effect of mounting level of stress experienced by people. In fact in today's life the problems related to stress have become so pervasive that it has become a major concern for scientists in various fields viz. medicine, neuro-biology, psychology, sociology, architecture and environmental sciences. Stress today has become so significant in everyone's life that a bulk of research in these fields is directly or indirectly concerned with the question of understanding the antecedent and consequences of stress and its management in such a way that quality of life of people may be improved.

A problem of such a magnitude requires that people develop a proper understanding of stress so that they may handle their own lives as well as those of others in a better way such that life for everyone concerned becomes healthier, more relaxed and productive. Insights developed by doctors, psycho-biologists, psychologists and even yoga practitioners can go a long way to help in this effort. Already people in various fields are working in close cooperation to develop an integrated approach to the problem of stress. This book is an attempt to provide a window through which a broad perspective about stress and its management can be obtained.

The idea behind writing this book is to help the reader to develop a proper understanding about stress and its implications. It is important to understand that all stress is not bad. Some thinkers even equate it with life in that having stress is a characteristic of living. Within a reasonable limit stress acts as a motive force to overcome obstacles and to solve problems. It is only when it becomes persistent or intense in magnitude that it has harmful consequences. If anticipated well in time much of it can be prevented. Where it cannot be prevented people can develop skills and abilities to handle it effectively. But before an attempt is made to study the implications of stress and its management, it is imperative that we have a clear picture of what stress is, why it occurs and how it is manifested.

What is Stress

Our psychobiological systems are programmed to work for the sake of survival. The theory of evolution propounded by Charles Darwin testifies to this fact. All our activities are directed at self-preservation which involves people struggling day in and day out for the sake of survival. For this there is a constant monitoring of internal states and external environments by the brain (which operates as its regulator) and whenever a situation occurs which involves risks to survival and well-being, corrective actions are taken. Most of the times these corrections are made automatically and we are not even consciously aware of them. At the most we may get the "OK" signals from within. As long as the corrections are taking place the person maintains the state of what is labelled as 'well-being'. When these automatic corrections are not possible there is a demand for some corrective action and the person does something to bring back the condition of 'no risk to survival'. As long as the effort remains within the range of routine activities, it does not affect the individual's well being. But when the routine action does not suffice to bring back the 'no risk' situation, an 'alert' signal is given and the organism/individual gets ready with an all out effort to face the eventuality. This all out response to a situation which can not be handled in a routine way, has been labelled as stress. In other words, we can say that when an individual's well being is threatened he undergoes certain psychological and physiological changes which prepare him to handle the threat through sustained activity. In the course of this preparation a set of complex activities take place which are an integral part of stress. These are described here.

Stress is a Drastic Response to a Drastic Situation

It is observed that no sooner than a person becomes aware of the threat or risk or pressure of the situation he becomes highly alert. His attention is totally focussed on the situation causing stress. Sometimes this focussing of attention is so much narrowed down that many important and relevant signals tend to be ignored. As a result the individual has to brace up to handle the situation and in the process undergoes strong emotional upheaval. The emotions experienced can be fear, anger, or agitation. And, if the person is asked to describe what is happening to him at that moment, he is likely to state that he is having tension or anxiety or he may label his state in terms of any one of the emotions that are appropriate to the situation. As an example we can quote here the words in which Arjun describes his own state before the 'Mahabharata' began.

> "My limbs fail, and my mouth is parched, my body quivers and my hair stands on end (seeing my kinsmen) the bow slips from hand, the skin burns and my mind is whirling around" (Says Arjun) Gita 1.20 & 1.30.

Stress involves Physiological Preparation

So far we have described the psychological aspects of stress. But underlying these psychological upheaval there is a great physiological preparation. The purpose of this is to equip the body to carry on sustained activity. It also equips the body to sustain itself if any physical injury takes place. The best evidence of such preparation comes from the works of Janis who showed that patients who described themselves as being under stress recovered faster and had less complications than those who were not stressed. A detailed analysis of the physiological condition of the individual undergoing stress shows that there is an increase in heart rate and blood pressure so that important chemicals are pumped faster into different parts of the body specially to the muscles. Digestion stops to economize on the blood supply which is required elsewhere. This condition continues so long as the individual continues his effort to manage the situation causing stress. Sometimes the response may be so severe or may persist so long that most of the energy of the body gets exhausted. You might have heard and seen how people on getting an extremely sad or a very happy news just collapse. Similarly, an experienced runner on seeing his adversary fast approaching the winning post may collapse on the ground. These are some examples of physical exhaustion due to stress.

Stress is a Generalized Response to all Types of Threat

It is a common observation that the threat to one's well-being can come from a variety of sources viz. viruses or bacteria, physical injury or possibility of failure in some important task. But irrespective of the nature of the threat the pattern of response remains the same at the physiological level, with some minor difference in the response of one individual from the other, but the response pattern for the same individual remains the same. Thus stress may be defined as a drastic response involving a set of complex activities taking place in an individual to meet a drastic situation. These activities may consist of a set of very specific, yet general psychological and physiological changes taking place in response to a threat. Stated more definitively, stress is a complex psychophysiological response to a situation which a person perceives to be beyond his coping capacity. Cognitively, it is experienced as a state of tension or turmoil and is often accompanied by anxiety. Physiologically it is a state of preparedness to tackle the danger inherent in the situation.

Stress and Stressors

The term stress is often used to denote tension or anxiety. Sometimes it is used to denote extra load of some sort also, in a sense similar to its use in physical sciences. But in psychology and other related fields its meaning has reversed. Now the term is used specifically for the *response of the organism* to an object or situation which causes stress. The stress causing object or situation itself is now termed as stressor. We can say that stress is the response to the stressor.

Any study of stress involves identifying a stressor and studying the individual's response to it. A stressor need not be a concrete object which is here and now. It can be an anticipated or imagined object or situation. For example, pre-examination or pre-operative stress are in anticipation of a situation. People sometimes imagine that an object poses threat and then experience stress in relation to that object. For instance, a girl may imagine that people do not like her and therefore she experiences stress.

To sum up, we can say that a stressor is any real, imagined, or anticipated object or situation which poses a threat to one's well-being and, stress is the response to it. It is important to state here that although theoretically any object or situation can be a stressor yet the same object may not always be a stressor. Often, stress depends upon the appraisal of the situation as a stressor by the person. For example, a worker may make a hell of his life by thinking that his boss is angry. The details of what all can cause stress and operate as stressors and how different factors operate to influence the impact of a stressor are detailed in the next chapter.

The Physiology of Stress Response

The state of tension or agitation experienced by a person during stress has an undercurrent of massive bodily activity. Hans Selye, the noted endocrinologist who has been the pioneer in the field of stress research showed that stress is a non specific primitive response of the body to any threat. He called it non-specific because whatever be the nature of threat, i.e., a wild animal, an attack of viruses in the body, a lost dream or a sense of guilt, the response remains the same. The complex changes which take place during stress response are shown in the box on page 7.

Bio-chemical Changes during stress
Increased arterial blood pressure
Increased heart rate
Increased flow of blood to 'active' muscles
Increased glucose level in blood
Increased Glucolysis in muscles
Increased mental activity

The response is also called General Adaptation Syndrome (GAS) because it helps in adapting to a stressor situation. Selye demonstrated that it is a three stage response (Fig. 1). The three phases of stress response are: the alarm stage, the stage of resistance and the stage of exhaustion. The three stages have their own specific characteristics.

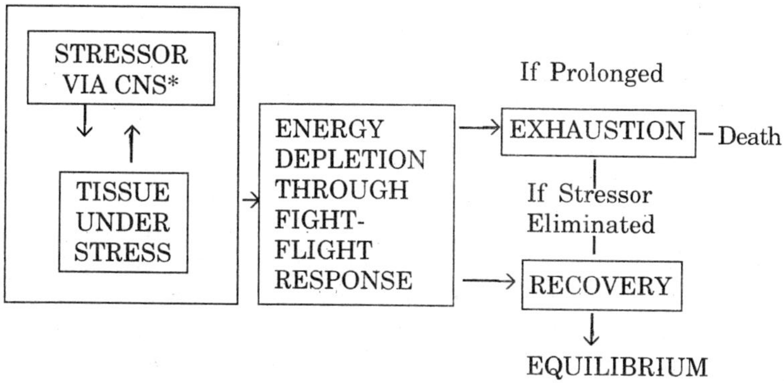

* Central Nervous System

Fig. 1: A Simple Depiction of Selye's Model

The Alarm Stage : This stage itself has two phases, the shock phase and the recovery phase. During the shock phase body functions get disturbed and there is an increase in heart rate and fall in muscle tone and the body temperature. Then, there is the recovery phase when there is full body preparedness to face the threat. A similar two phase psychological response is also observed. During the shock phase an individual is dazed and disoriented. Gradually he recovers, takes stock of the situation and decides upon the strategies to cope with stress.

The Stage of Resistance : During this second stage the resources mobilized during the first stage are utilized to adapt to the stressor situation. At this stage efficiency is high and the organism is able to resist the stressor. But because of the fight put up in resisting the stressor the energy available gradually gets depleted, leading to the third stage of stress response viz. the stage of exhaustion.

The Stage of Exhaustion : At this stage resources are completely depleted, the organisms is not able to fight the stressor and illness or death may occur. Fortunately, most of the time we manage the stressors without reaching the third stage. This is how we live through the problems that we encounter every moment of life and come out of them wiser and more experienced.

How Stress Response is Regulated

As already stated stress is a complex psychobiological response involving almost every system of the body. This response is regulated by the brain which operates like the manager of any complex organization in the corporate world. It gets signals about the various situations in the environment or within the organisms, and interprets them in different ways. These responses could be interpreted as 'neutral' or benign with no need to react or as challenging with expectation of positive results through action or as a risky situation causing a threat with need to initiate emergency actions. Depending on the interpretation made, subsequent signals are sent out to various parts of the nervous system and the special glands called endocrine glands. Certain chemicals are then released from these glands which regulate the activities of the various organs of the body. The most important among the chemicals released are adrenaline, nor-adrenaline and the cortico-steroids. In addition to the chemicals released by the endocrine glands certain chemicals are released by the brain also which carry messages to the body and other parts of the brain. These chemicals help in triggering of the stress response as also in slowing down or tapering off the response so that it is not revived if the same stressor appears again. When a chemical, psychological or behavioural response (also known as coping) to a stress occurs the brain gets a feed back via sensory inputs or through the chemicals circulating in the brain. These feed backs help in deciding whether to prolong, stop or modify the response.

CHAPTER 2

SOURCES OF STRESS

If stress has to be prevented or minimised, it requires that the sources of stress be identified so that either these sources or the response to them may be appropriately modified. This chapter presents an overview of the sources of stress. The list is in no way exhaustive yet it can give a general idea about these sources.

The Stressor and the Stress

It has already been stated in Chapter 1 that the term 'stressor' refers to the stimulus situations that cause 'stress' and stress refers to the psychophysiological response to it. These stressors could be concrete objects or abstract things like somebody's demeaning remark, a feeling of loneliness, a failure in one's endeavours etc. Also a stressor need not be something that is 'here' and 'now', for it can even be anticipated or imagined, viz., an approaching examination and apprehension that one might fail. Although the terms 'stressor' and the 'sources of stress' are used interchangeably, no object is universally a stressor.

When Does a Stimulus become a Stressor

Stress is a response of an organism to a situation that threatens the well-being of a person. These situations could be simple sensory inputs like extremes of heat or cold, or major catastrophic events like an earthquake or riot, yet no stimulus is a stressor for everyone all the time. This is because stress depends on whether a particular object or situation is posing a threat to an individual or not. For example, a man who has nothing to lose is not threatened by burglars. Similarly, a person who can cope with a situation or at least feels that he can cope with it does not feel threatened by it. Here cultural conditioning also plays a significant role. In any culture, people develop different values, concepts and perceptions about different objects. In other words, a person's worldview is by and large culturally determined, and in this way defines as to which objects are benign or threatening. For example, separation from a family is more threatening in societies like India where people are not trained to be independent. This may not be so in cultures where people are emancipated from dependency at an early age. Similarly, while for a Westerner, leisure is a source of satisfaction, for an average Japanese it becomes a stressor. Similarly, a person brought up under conditions of hardship may not consider hard work stressful.

A stressor need not be a real object because one can react to an anticipated or imagined situation also. When a person experiences stress before an examination, interview or a forthcoming board meeting, he is reacting to the anticipation of a stressor. But a young woman who is constantly experiencing stress because she thinks she is too fat, too thin or ugly is reacting to an imagined stressor. Such stressors are very commonly experienced in social situations where one often does not know what the other person thinks and many such stressors may be seen as emanating from 'the other person'. Situations like 'he hates me' or 'has designs against me' are other examples of imagined stressors.

All these stressors can come either from the physical environment in which man lives or they may emanate from his psychological and social world. Illustrations of the stressors from the two sets of environments are given here under.

A. Stressors in the Physical Environment

We live and work in an environment that comprises of a variety of physical, chemical and biological conditions that become sources of stress, leading to adverse consequences. There is a need to understand these conditions because their existence and prevalence in any situation can be a cause of various psychological and physical symptoms like decreased efficiency, lack of satisfaction and loss of physical and mental health. Some of these environmental conditions, even if they are not causing stress, may increase vulnerability to various stressor-like substances that have toxic or harmful effects that can disturb an individual's well-being. These substances can also lead to perception of the situations that can be a source of stress, as knowledge about their harmful effect can create anxiety and insecurity. Organic solvents of various types, for example hydrocarbons, carbon monoxide and carbon disulphide, heavy metals, pesticides and various aromatic compounds are examples of such toxic substances. These chemicals tend to adversely affect a person's psychological and physical functioning. It has been established that exposure to carbon monoxide leads to symptoms like unusual fatigue, lack of energy, irritability, impairment of cognitive functions and disturbances in manual dexterity and eye-hand coordination.

Constant exposure to noise is one of the several curses of modern day living. Our lives are tainted by aircraft noise or by the noise of driving vehicles, machines, human speech, loud sounds emanating from audio-systems of various types and to top it all the noise from the loudspeakers, in the name of music or public awareness campaigns. Noise can be intermittent or continuous. Researches show that intermittent noise is more stressful than a continuous noise leading to lowered performance and annoyance. The effects of noise depend on the nature of work also. When a person is engaged in doing monotonous work, noise becomes more stressful. Like noise, vibrations can also cause stress. Workers operating machines and tools using compressed air and those working on railway trains are exposed to prolonged vibrations. A variety of ill-affects of exposure to vibrations have been identified. These include chest pain, stomach pain, and pain in hands and joints. Often numbness of hands can also occur.

Human beings can function optimally when they are exposed to a limited range of temperatures. Temperatures beyond a certain range or extremes of temperature specially that on the high side have adverse effect on people. The effect of atmospheric temperature depends upon the climate, humidity, air circulation, clothing and the nature of work one is doing. During extremes of temperature the body has to work hard to keep itself within the optimal range of temperature and this effort can cause fatigue and loss of well-being.

Pathogens and viruses are biological stressors that when inside the body cause an activation causing stress and subsequently illness. As long as the body can fight these stressors it continues to resist occurrence of illnesses. A prolonged exposure to these pathogens and the inability of the body to fight them can lead to exhaustion and various illnesses.

B. Psychological Stressors

The other group of stressors usually known as psychological stressors become stressors because of their meaning for an individual. Psychological stressors cause stress through the cognitive interpretation of the situation as a source of threat. These stressors are called psychological stressors because their capacity to cause stress depends upon their subjective interpretation or appraisal and not on the objective situation. The role of subjective appraisal can be appreciated well if we consider the fact that very often people deliberately get into a situation that, from an objective point of view, is generally thought of as threatening. Sky-diving and bungee jumping are examples of such situations that are appraised by some people as challenging and exciting rather than threatening and therefore instead of finding these situations stressful they get a thrill out of these activities. On the other hand many harmless situations like a dental examination act as stressors because they are perceived as a threat to well-being. The perception of threat to well-being can emanate from anticipation of harm, losses, frustrations and through unusual body sensations.

Harmful situations involve realistic possibilities of some physical damage like injury or loss of life. A life-threatening disease, a major surgery, an encounter with a dangerous animal are among such situations that can keep people constantly under stress. A threat of harm may not relate to only physical harm, it can also relate to one's reputation or social relationships. Losses that cause stress could be the loss of a concrete object or it could be the loss of prestige, status, a relationship or even that of a dream. Loss of a familiar surrounding can also be a source of stress, for example, when a person moves from one place to another or from one position to the other he feels threatened because he has to give a new meaning to every stimulus in the situation. It is in such situations that there is what is called 'culture shock', when old learning becomes redundant and new things have to be learnt. Because of the same reasons, a new job or a new position in the hierarchy or any other major change becomes a stressor. Loss of a relationship or of an object of love are stressors because they become part of the self. Frustrations are the most common sources of stress. Frustration refers to a situation in which some important need is prevented from being satisfied. This situation is also often termed 'blocked goal' situation. The degree of stress depends upon the intensity of need and its significance for the person as well as on the source of frustration. Some of these sources can be beyond one's control and a person may decide to live with them. In other situations he may persist with efforts to overcome the frustration. Under such circumstances the stress is likely to persist. Identification of the source of frustration can help to eliminate stress. Frustration can come from the external circumstances and natural events like rain, storm or floods. Other external sources of frustration are social taboos and restrictions. Society puts certain restrictions on its members to help in its smooth functioning.

When these restrictions interfere with the satisfaction of any need of a person, they become a source of frustration. Poverty is a common source of frustration, because it deprives a person of satisfying many needs. Internal sources of frustration have been identified as unrealistic goal setting, rigid morals, values and conflict and personal inadequacy to

Fig. 1. Unrealistic goal setting as a source of stress

deal with situations. Many a times frustrations originate in unrealistic goal setting. Often people set a goal so high that it cannot be achieved in reality but there is a constant striving to attain the unattainable leading to repeated frustrations.

Frustrations can also occur when goals cannot be achieved because of one's moral values. Refusing to compromise with one's set of values like being against giving or taking bribes or going out of the way to serve the interests of influential persons may cost him dearly in terms of being deprived from rightful benefits and in the process cause frustration. Source of frustration may also lie in situations of conflicts. A conflict situation is defined as a situation in which more than one response tendency is aroused. Conflicts may arise either because of two opposite forces acting in the situation or because of two different goals evoking incompatible response tendencies. Wishing to do something and at the same time not wanting to do it is a situation representing conflict. The most famous and well-known example of conflict can be cited from Mahabharata when Arjun standing on the battle field facing the Kauravas is not able to decide whether to swallow the insults and humiliation caused by them to the Pandavas or to fight his own kinsmen in the Kauravas.

Conflict as a Source of Stress

Standing in the warfield of Kurukshetra Arjun ready to fight, experienced extreme guilt and is frozen, seeing that enemies are none but his own teachers and relatives. The person here (Arjun) at the same time desires to attain and not to attain the goal.

The Holy Gita 1.28-47

Hamlet's dilemma in the Shakespeare's Play 'Hamlet' is another well-known illustration of the conflict situation. Ambiguous situations are another source of stress. Very often we encounter stimuli that can be interpreted in many ways and one is not sure as to which interpretation is the correct one. Situations like these that do not give one clear message are ambiguous and they put pressures/demands for vigilant search for cues to validate one's interpretation. These pressures/demands cause stress. In social situations when behaviours of other persons provide ambiguous cues, or when no feedback is available severe anxiety leading to stress is experienced. It is not uncommon for a student to experience such ambiguous situations producing stress when his teachers give comments like "you have done well but there is scope for improvement".

Situations of both overload and underload can also be a source of frustration. While the situation of overload is defined in terms of demands to handle excess of information, the underload is the absence of any demand from the environment. Overload is seen as either quantitative, that is, too much to do or qualitative that is, too difficult a task. For example of task overload see box A

Box A – Examples of Task overload

(a) too many stimuli to be handled at a time
(b) stimuli to be handled are too complex
(c) complex instructions to be followed
(d) task to be done at a fast pace

Underload, on the other hand, occurs in situations where there is minimal handling of information. Tasks that are repetitive, routine, boring or done in under-stimulating working environment are examples of situations of underload. Situations of task underload are summarised in box B.

Box B – Examples of Task underload

(a) handling of minimal information
(b) repetitive work
(c) prolonged waiting for a demand to occur
(d) situations of social isolation and confinement

Most individuals prefer to function under condition of a range of optimal load. Beyond this range both overload as well as underload become a source of stress as in both the situations an individual has to make extra effort to bring his functioning at an optimal level. In situations of overload one either cuts down on demands or makes extra effort to keep pace with the demands. Under conditions of underload, on the contrary one has to create an extra load to bring it to an optimal level.

One may get unusual sensations from within which act as stressors because they do not fall within the range of everyday experiences. Aches and pains, distensions, tingling, strange odours or sounds (e.g. hearing sounds) are among such sensations. The fact that such sensations force people to seek help can give an idea about the extent of stress caused by them. Shamans and quacks often take advantage of such a stress and exploit the gullible people. To the above list one can include negative emotions like anxiety and guilt that cause unpleasant states causing stress.

Adjustment Demands and Stress: Stressor Events

Upto this point we have dwelt upon discrete stimuli that can act as stressors. In real life situations, however, stressors do not normally appear as discrete stimuli. Our lives comprise of complex events which upset the smooth flow of life because they put demands for adjustment in almost every aspect of life. These events may occur as major happenings, personal events or as minor day-to-day happenings that act as constant irritants. The nature and impact of such events in terms of stress caused differ in several ways.

Major happenings or cataclysmic events occur in the form of large scale catastrophies influencing the lives of many people. Floods, cyclones, earthquakes, riots or 'building fires' fall in this category. Since these events occur all of a sudden, people are not prepared for them. Hence, their impact is greater than that of other stressors. Catastrophies cause severe physical, psychological and social trauma. For example, an earthquake or a building fire may cause physical injury, loss of property and personal belongings as well as loss of many near and dear ones. Although many people are able to cope with these events with unusual control over their reactions and very often these events bring out the best in human nature as the people get more concerned about the welfare of others, yet they still are a source of stress. Personal stressors are commonly known as life events. Such events happen to a single individual at a point of time and they can occur in everyone's life. Life events put a demand for major adjustments and are therefore source of stress. Marriage, promotion in job or transfer means adjustment to a new life style, to a new set of people and a different set of commitments. Other such life events are deaths (of a near one), births, moves, loss of job etc. Holmes and Rahe have done pioneering work in the area of stress due to life events. Through their researches they have demonstrated that such life events have a predictable stressor's impact on people's lives and this impact can be expressed in quantitative terms. Another set of events are more chronic and they drag on in the life of a person (Fig. 2).

We may call this set of events, chronic stressors. While some of these stressors may be persistent viz. overcrowded and noisy homes, others may occur as daily hassles that quickly replace one another. These events/stressors act as minor irritants and have a cumulative impact on demands of day-to-day living. Shortage, sudden strikes by various people, traffic jams are examples of some such stresses. Our lives

Fig. 2. Daily hassels like family fights act as constant irritant

have some pleasant happenings also and they negate the impact of daily hassles. We call these pleasant happenings, daily uplifts.

To sum up stress can come from a variety of sources both environmental as well as personal. They do not cause equally severe stress in every one. Many factors interact with one another to determine the severity of stress experienced by a person. These factors form the subject matter of the next chapter.

CHAPTER 3

DIFFERENTIAL EXPERIENCE OF STRESS

The variety of conditions which are stress producing have been reviewed in the previous chapter. The stress caused by these conditions, however, is not equally severe all the time for everyone. The same stressor may come and go without any serious consequences or it may cause a severe upheaval in one's psychological and physiological functioning. The concept of differential experiences of stress refers to these variations in the extent to which a stressful situation has an adverse effect on an individual's functioning. Since prevention and control of stress is possible only when the factors causing it are identified, their identification becomes important.

You will appreciatc that the severity of stress is the outcome of a complex interaction between an individual's appraisal of the situation, the characteristics of the stressor itself and the stress tolerance of an individual. However, these factors so complexly interact with each other that it is difficult to point one's finger at any one cause. For example, when a senior manager in a factory gets a heart attack during a workers' strike it is very difficult to say whether it is due to a blow to his ego, overwork or due to being let down by his most trusted lieutenants A proper understanding is therefore required for the variations in the severity of stress experienced by an individual; these are discussed under three broad headings, i.e. the stressor characteristics, individual differences, in vulnerability and coping resources.

Stressor Characteristics and the Severity of Stress

The stressor characteristics that determine the severity of stress experienced in a given situation are the stressor significance, its timing, duration and multiplicity. Situations that involve frustration of some important needs are stress producing. But since these needs vary in their significance for any one, the relative stress caused by them also varies. For example, a loss causes more stress than any other situation. The loss of a child is the most poignant experience for any one since it upsets the meaning of life itself. A child symbolises hopes and dreams for its parents. These are lost when a child dies. Situations like serious illness, jail term and demotion in the job are other such situations that singly cause frustration of several important needs.

Any stressor that persists over a long duration can have more serious repercussions than a stressor that comes and goes after a short duration. A persistent stressor becomes more irritating (therefore stress producing) if it cannot be controlled. Take for example a loud noise; if it persists uncontrolled, it becomes quite irritating. Many stress producing circumstances in life are unending or occur repeatedly to act as chronic stressor. Working on a monotonous job, living in an overcrowded home, adverse financial conditions or unemployment are some examples of stressors having a persistent character. These stressors demand continuous efforts to manage them that in itself becomes a source of stress.

Observations on soldiers during war have shown that the longer a soldier is in the field the more adverse is the effect. If a single stressor can cause stress of a severe intensity imagine what havoc can be caused when more than one stressor is affecting some one at a particular time. Each stressor makes its own demands. These demands get multiplied when several stressors come together. For example, taking up a new job is stressful for anyone. But if someone takes up a new job in a new place, borrows a large sum of money and finds the new neighbourhood uncongenial, the situation is likely to be highly stress-producing for him.

Severity of stress also increases as the actual time for the stressor event approaches. Every student knows how stress related symptoms become prominent as the examination time approaches. Similarly, it is noticed among novice parachutists that as the time for the actual jump comes near, the stress is at its highest and disappears as soon as the jump is taken.

A similar shift in anxiety which is an aspect of stress is noted in examinations. Students feel maximum anxiety immediately before the examination and then it disappears as they start writing (Fig. 1).

OH GOD THE EXAM IS ABOUT TO BEGIN AND I STILL HAVE TO REVISE THIS CHAPTER!

Fig. 1. Pressure as a source of stress.

Most stressful situations cause more severe stress in a grown up person than in children. One reason for this is that the nervous system of children is more resilient allowing them to recover faster.

The second reason why stress is less severe in childhood is that children are not in a position to understand the implications of the various situations in life and therefore, do not feel threatened by them. Maternal deprivation however, is an exception because it acts as a multiple stressor. It also deprives children of the opportunity to learn about stress management. Finally, the qualities responsible for affecting the severity of stress are its controllability and predictability. The stressor that can be controlled by an individual is less stressful than the one that cannot be controlled. For example, when a dentist tells his patient to signal if he wants the dentist to stop the painful procedure the treatment is less stressful than when no such freedom is allowed. In work situations we can think of a top executive who sits late in the office and gets satisfaction out of it while the peon waiting on him feels stressed because his prolonged stay is decided by his boss.

Similarly, when we know about a coming event and are therefore ready for it stress caused by it is less severe. Death of a person after a prolonged illness is taken into the stride more easily than death due to some sudden cause.

Characteristics of the stressor alone do not determine the severity of stress experienced. Vulnerability of an individual also plays an important part. Their role is discussed in the next section.

Individual Differences in Vulnerability to Stress

Upto this point we have been concerned with the stressor qualities that decide the severity of stress experienced by an individual's collapse under a particular stressful situation while others may take it in their stride. A question may be asked how in a community where most of the circumstances are the same for everyone it is only a small number of people who fall sick repeatedly? How do we explain the fact that people who belong to lower class experience more stress and suffer more adverse consequences of stress? To answer such questions we have to look at those characteristics and circumstances that determine individual differences in vulnerability or resistance to stress.

Many of these characteristics are an outcome of the day to day learning. Such learning may take place either through conditioning of which one is not aware, or it may be learning that occurs as cognition and skills that develop in the process of coping with life's many problems. To this may be added certain personality traits whose presence makes an individual stress-resistant. Lastly, the total circumstances prevailing at the time when the stressor event occurs influence how severe the stress will be. All these factors and their impact are discussed below.

Learning and Stress

Psychologists are gradually agreeing with the idea that learning plays an important role in determining an individual's stress tolerance. Problems and threats are a part of life. We encounter them every moment of our life but we are not always falling victim to them simply because through our experience we learn to take them in our stride. In the course of development we get habituated to them, develop an understanding about their transitory nature or most importantly we learn to cope with them.

Habituation takes place through a special type of learning known as conditioning, i.e. when we encounter same or similar situations repeatedly, we stop responding to them. In technical jargon the stress response undergoes extinction. Extinction serves an economical function. Life would be difficult if we do not get habituated to stressors like unpleasant odours, sights or sounds, to people we do not like, to pain and misery. Through habituation our life gets easier than it would be if we constantly got irritated by them.

Besides habituation we also develop skills for handling various stressful situations. Every successful endeavour adds to our competency to cope with stress. Interestingly, an awareness that we have such competency by itself reduces the severity of stress experienced.

A third form of learning responsible for reducing stress takes place at the cognitive level, i.e. a repeated encounter with stressor and success in coping with them makes one realise that hard times do not last forever. This realization or insight comes through reflection and logical analysis of various encounters with stressful situations. Once gained such an insight protects one against stress. As one grows up one also develops a way of looking at difficult situations. The way one looks at these situations or appraises them influences one's vulnerability. The role of appraisal in stress vulnerability is explained in the next paragraph.

Appraisal and Vulnerability

Before taking any action one makes an appraisal of the total situation. A situation may or may not be appraised as threatening. Even if it is appraised as threatening the threat involved may vary from mild to severe. The stress experienced tends to be related to threat perceived. An interview may be fun or may involve high stakes in terms of its being of life time significance. In the latter case the anticipation of failure is a threat therefore stressful but not so in case of the former. Whenever we talk of psychological factors in stress, we are referring to perceptions about the situation in which an experience takes place. The other important factor responsible for variations in the experience of stress is the personality of the individual.

Personality and Stress

Although personality characteristics differ among individuals, these are basically differences in their reactivity therefore they also influence their vulnerability to stress. Evidence for such variations among individuals came to light with the works of Thurlow. Spread over a period of ten years his researches showed that in any community there are a small number of persons who fall sick repeatedly. These are the people with high susceptibility to illness. This high illness susceptibility is thought to be due to their personality makeup. People with high reactivity are likely to suffer more because of stress as is evident from the high incidence of illness in this group of people. A brief discussion of the personality characteristics that contribute to an individual's vulnerability to stress could help in better understanding of this.

Locus of Control

By now you should know that the belief that one controls whatever happens to him is a great source of strength whereas the belief that things are beyond one's control is highly demoralising. These beliefs emanate from a stable characteristics of personality known as Locus of Control. Some people believe that the outcome of whatever they do depends on their own efforts. These people know for sure that if they work for something success is bound to come and if they achieve something they give credit to themselves. These people have been given the term 'Internals' because they believe that the locus of control lies within themselves. On the other extreme are the people who are called 'Externals'.

These people are fatalistic in their outlook and believe that the outcome of any situation depends not on their efforts but on luck, chance or on powerful "others". The 'Internals' have higher stress tolerance. They are able to approach various problems with greater confidence and therefore are able to keep their stress level low. The 'Externals' on the other hand suffer from a sense of helplessness and have a greater susceptibility to stress because of their non-fighting attitude towards the problems they encounter.

A/B Type Personalities

These personality types were first observed by two cardiologists Rosenman and Fridman. In the course of working with coronary heart disease (CHD) these cardiologists discovered that in people who develop heart disease a typical behaviour pattern is followed, to this they gave the name Type A behaviour pattern. And the people showing this pattern were Type A persons. To differentiate the other group, i.e., the ones not showing Type A behaviour, they were called Type B persons or persons with Type B behaviour pattern.

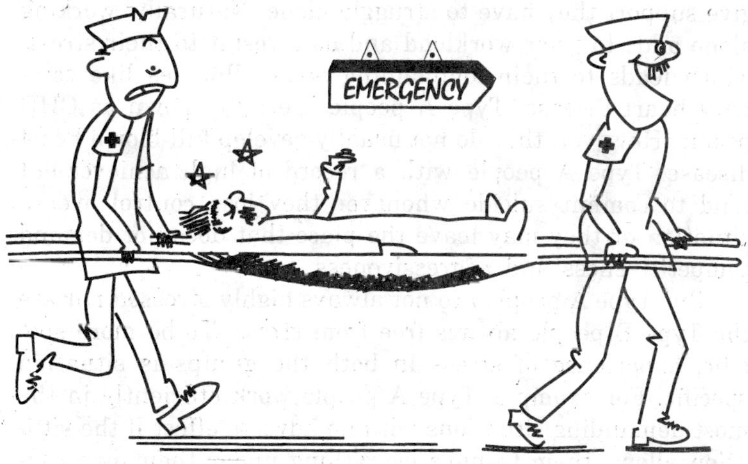

HE ACTED SO HARD ON ALL STRESS-PREVENTION ADVICE GIVEN BY THE DOCTOR THAT HE IS NOW DOWN WITH EXHAUSTION

Fig. 2. Self generated stress in Type A persons

Type A persons have a strong need for achievement which is manifested in their being highly competitive with an unusual sense of time urgency. They are in a constant hurry and are recognised by their vigorous speech and impatience. Type B persons on the other hand, do not show such a strong need for achievement and therefore do not show the characteristics that mark the Type A persons. Type B persons are relatively relaxed and contented. The behaviour of Type A people is stress generating (Fig. 2) as they react aggressively to situations that are uncontrollable or if the situation is controlled by someone else. In such situations they feel threatened and so become restless and hostile. They go out of their way to gain control over the situation.

Because of these characteristics Type A people go on adding stress to their lives. For example, in job situations they get over-involved with their jobs, are often unhappy with their colleagues and are grumbling about their subordinates. Dissatisfied with everyone's work they go on adding to their own workload till it becomes overwhelming. A natural fallout of all this is that others start resenting these hyper-reactive Type A people. Because no one is willing to give support they have to struggle alone. Naturally, working alone adds to their workload and as a result to their stress, which leads to their complaining about illnesses like coronary heart disease. Type A people are also known as CHD people. However, they do not usually develop full-blown heart disease. Type A people with a record of high achievement tend to commit suicide whenever they lose control over a situation or they may leave the place that does not demand competitiveness and aggressiveness.

But Type A people are not always highly stressed nor are the Type B people always free from stress. To be more specific, experience of stress in both the groups is situation specific. For example, Type A people work efficiently in the most demanding situations with no adverse effect if the situation allows them to have everything under their own control. Similarly, Type B people get upset if the situation demands that they exert a full control over it. Reactions of the two types of people differ in social situations also. Type B people can adjust with a variety of people but Type A persons are not comfortable with their own tribe. Even in the marital life they are alright with a Type B spouse.

The Hardy Personality

Cobasa, an expert in the field of stress has identified a cluster of traits that when present make an individual stress resistant. To this he has given the name 'the Hardy Personality'. Cobasa and his colleagues identified people who remain healthy even after going through severe stress. They found that these people differ from others in terms of certain beliefs, attitudes and action tendencies. The characteristics that mark such people are termed control, commitment and challenge. Control refers to having a belief that one can control the outcome of events rather than feel helpless when faced with a difficult situation. Because of this quality people with a sense of control come undisturbed out of the most demanding situations.

Commitment refers to a tendency to get involved in life's ongoing events rather than being a passive on looker. Hardy people actively participate in life's drama during both happy events as well as during unhappy events. When disaster comes they may be the first ones to initiate the rescue operations and take charge of things rather than wait for other people to order or to initiate action.

Challenge as defined by Cobasa refers to the belief that change rather than stability is the order of life so be ready for it. Because of this belief hardy people are willing to take into their stride whatever change may occur. Other workers in the field of stress agree that ability to see life as a cycle of change and accept the challenge presented by the various happenings gives them strength to withstand stresses of various sort.

All the three dimensions describe a fighting attitude towards life and ensure that individuals come out healthy after experiencing stress. Hardy persons function as responsible citizens, parents, or employees and are the ones who accept life as it is. The three dimensions, i.e. control, commitment and challenge are all related to an active coping style about which you will know more from the chapter on coping.

Coping Resources

By coping resources we mean those resources that help in coping with a stressful situation. While some of these resources are obtained from the external environment viz., material aids, other supportive people etc., there are also other resources that come from within the person. Health, morale and positive self-concept and certain beliefs and attitudes facilitate tolerance, therefore, act as resources. It should be clear that mere existence of resources is not enough. High tolerance for stress comes from the assurance that one's resources are adequate. When coping resources are judged as adequate there is no stress, when the resources are seen as somewhat inadequate the situation poses a challenge and the severity of stress increases as the resources get inadequate. Because resources vary from one situation to another, severity of stress also varies. A person may be able to handle the most drastic situations at one time but get upset by a minor incident some other time. A surgeon may rip open the chest of hundreds of patients, confident that he can handle the situation successfully but may get upset on seeing his own small child crying when bruised.

Health and Morale

The fact that stress is non-normal condition of the individual makes it essential that one remains in good health to be able to tolerate or fight back the problems so that they do not cause any severe stress. It goes without saying that compared to a weakling a robust person has more energy at his disposal. For him the state of exhaustion will not come so fast as to allow stress to have an upper hand. Observations of people during situations of disaster, illness or surgery provide good evidence that healthy people fare far better in situations generating a high level of stress. The same holds true in work situations also where people who are in good physical and mental health experience lesser stress than those who are in poor health. Morale is closely related to the health of a person. It refers to a condition in which a person feels confident about his strength and capability. Morale acts like an internal programme which monitors the resources then gives the command: "Resources adequate: keep the fight going". Reports of the two World Wars, specially of the survivors of the Nazi Concentration Camps have demonstrated that those who were able to come out of all the agony unscathed were the ones with high morale. A belief in God and in one's inner strength, hope of getting out of the stressful situation and the knowledge that others are concerned with his welfare are factors that keep a person's morale high. Value of morale becomes convincingly evident from the findings of the health scientists. People fall ill or die when they are so demoralised that they stop fighting to overcome the problems in life. George Engell has given this condition the name of 'giving-up given-up' syndrome. Others have labelled it as the state of helplessness. A little encouragement or hope or support can raise a person's morale and also reverse the course of stress. It will be worthwhile to refer here an actual case in support of this point.

P. Lal, a noted Indian literary figure on one of his visits to USA fell seriously ill and had to be admitted in the hospital. When his condition deteriorated his family was summoned from India. As he was struggling between life and death, shunting between consciousness and coma, his family and the doctors waited wistfully for the end to come. One night when he came round from his coma, he saw someone in his room. He strained hard to find out who she was and what was she doing. Gradually, it dawned on him that she was his nurse, whispering and praying for his survival. He told himself, P. Lal writes, "Look here in a strange country a stranger is wishing and praying for my survival and I am waiting for death. No, I must live." This raised his morale. Gradually he recovered from his illness and was well enough to write about this in his autobiography. People use small anchors to keep their morale high, a sweet memory, a future task, a meaning in one's experiences, all these can be used to keep the morale high.

Skills and Knowledge

Stressful situations are basically problem situations that require certain skills and understanding about them so that they can be handled effectively. The knowledge needed could be of the resources required to handle a particular situation and from where to obtain them. This knowledge can comprise of simple thumb rules like first-aid rules, human-relation rules or fire-fighting rules, or of the details of manoeuvring of complex gadgets. The same thing applies to the skills also. Since a major chunk of stressors come from social situations and because many resources can be obtained from other people, communication and interpersonal skills are the most important ones needed to deal with situations. Both these skills are closely related.

Communication skills consist of the skill in selecting appropriate language for a situation and of using it effectively. If a person has developed skill in the use of written language he has an added advantage since the ability to read and write provides an access to a variety of other resources while an illiterate person has to depend on others. This fact can explain why literacy is considered the single most powerful means of empowering any group of people. Equally important are the social skills that equip a person to successfully handle various social situations. Social skills help a person to establish satisfying interpersonal relationships. Stress reducing skills include skill in making a correct assessment about the other person, ability to see the situation from the other person's point of view so that the other person knows what ideas and attitudes are being communicated as it is from the feedback only that the person will know whether his message is understood or not. For example, if 'A' cuts a joke, 'B' should understand A's intention and the context of the joke and communicate through laughing that he has enjoyed the joke. Similarly 'A' should be able to ensure that the particular joke will be understood by 'B' and would not hurt his feelings. When an individual lacks in any one of these skills, he experiences severe anxiety in social situations, lacks self-assertion and gets isolated. Conversely, a person having these skills is sure of himself and therefore experiences less stress in social situations.

Belief as a Resource

Beliefs are at the core of all our cognitions that regulate our appraisal of the various situations. Some of our beliefs condition our outlook towards life and help in reducing the experience of stress/threat. Belief in God, or in the possibility that various situations and their outcome can be controlled, and belief in one's capabilities, all help in keeping one's stress level low. Belief in God helps to keep a person's morale up and therefore reduces anxiety. Whenever people are carrying on a struggle, they coin slogans stating positive ideas. The value of such slogans lies in the fact that they reinforce positive beliefs in one's own capabilities. A belief that the outcome of a situation can be controlled helps a person to have a fighting attitude towards a stressful situation taken as a challenge rather than a threat. Belief in one's capabilities amounts to having a positive self-concept. People with a positive self-concept are more confident, are enthused with energy, can maintain high morale and therefore, can tolerate stress to a greater extent.

Social Support

The support available to a person in times of stress is among the most important of resources. Even the knowledge that other people are available helps to keep the stress level low. A supportive person can help by making a more objective assessment of the situation as well as in the actual coping process by providing assistance in handling the stressful situation. For example, when a worker is harassed the entire work-force is ready to fight for his rights. Other ways in which a supportive person helps is by giving information and guidance or by providing material help.

More than resources, an individual's perception about their presence or absence provides a key to the problem of stress. When individuals feel that they have adequate resources their perceptions about the entire situation change since they see it as a 'situation under control'. The building up of these resources is the result of a lifetime process. As an individual grows up, interacts with various significant people and copes with various stressful situations he also builds up his resources. For example, a person brought-up in a warm and supportive family environment where discipline is balanced by encouragement, will in all probability, have self confidence and a positive self-concept. Added to this if there have been experiences of personal success and there are also role models who take failures and disappointments in their stride there is every possibility of this person developing an outlook towards life marked by hope and faith.

Contrary to this, persons brought up in homes full of tensions do not get a similar opportunity. On the contrary these persons may build up a high level of anxiety that in itself is stress producing. Likewise, people who have lived a life full of hardships and privations cannot be expected to have a sense of mastery, develop skills or emotional richness to counteract the adverse effect of stress. Exposure to religion also influences one's stress tolerance in different ways. If religion develops faith in God and imbibes hope it acts as a resource but if it leads to fatalism, it results in a sense of helplessness and thus, adds to the severity of stress.

Irrespective of resources the social circumstances in which stress occurs also determine the stress tolerance. When everyone is suffering together and coping together, as it happens in a disaster situation like a flood or an earthquake, stress often tends to have even a positive effect. In such disaster situations often conflicts and differences are forgotten and even psychological symptoms disappear as people are making a positive and worthwhile contribution towards a worthwhile task of common interest. Similarly, if everyone is working hard in a highly demanding job situation, people do not generally complain of the situation being stressful. An important operating factor causing stress is the legitimacy of the demand causing stress. When demands put by a person or the situation is considered justified, stress experienced is not so severe. For example, in the case of childbirth, though there is an extra burden put on the mother but the mother is able to carry on with her job of caring for the baby without any adverse psychological or another adverse effect.

CHAPTER 4

AFTER EFFECTS OF STRESS

The reactions to a stressful situation are manifested in a variety of responses at physiological and psychological level. The most important among these responses is coping or the efforts to control the stress. When situations are unpredictable or are such that cannot be controlled or coped with, stress continues for long and causes various disturbances in a person's functioning. Such disturbances occur only when coping efforts fail or have to be continued over a longer period. Disturbances of this kind occur only if the demands put by a situation are so overwhelming that one cannot manage them with normal efforts or if the resources required for managing the stressful situation are so inadequate that the person cannot handle it. The adverse consequences of such prolonged stress have been named aftereffects of stress. A brief overview of these after effects is being presented here.

Stress and Cognition

The most important among changes induced in a person's functioning due to stress are noted in cognitions. These effects are important because our cognitions are the first link in the chain of events that take place in response to a stimulus. Naturally the way we perceive a situation, use our experience to understand it and to manage it, decides what residual effect a stressful experience will leave.

While reacting to a situation we first receive information about it through our senses, interpret it, store it in our memory and then recall it when required. All these processes are encapsulated in the term cognition. Cognitive appraisal is fundamental in our adjustment to a situation since the appropriateness of our response to the world depends upon a reasonably objective appraisal of the situation. This objectivity is often lost under stress. The process through which it occurs is described in the following paragraphs.

Stress Affects our Attention

When facing a threatening situation like a gnawing pain, a predator, an adversary or a problem at hand we tend to focus our total attention on the most important aspect of the situation. The 'total attention' is paid to the most relevant cues. It also has an adaptive value though it may not always lead to adaptation. Under stress 'attention' gets narrowed. Let's see how stress operates to narrow down attention.

When an individual becomes aware of a threat, widespread physiological changes take place as part of the stress response. These responses are cognitively interpreted as negative emotions that demand attention, and extra effort is put to concentrate on the most important cues. A natural fallout of this activity is that many other important cues are lost sight of. (Haven't you ever ignored signals of hunger or fatigue while concentrating on a highly demanding situation?) From a review of studies of peripheral vision the psychologist D.E. Broadbent concludes that when people under stress are made to respond to a set of lights, heat or noise, they tend to ignore the peripheral signals and under sleep deprivation they ignore the central cues and respond to peripheral signals. This phenomenon explains what is often termed error of judgement in various accidents. Working under stress machine operators often lose sight of important danger signals, and students often complain that they could not read or simply misread instructions and thus spoilt their examination papers. Since examinations are high stress situations, such perceptual error due to narrowing of attention is always possible.

Stress Influences Memory

Memory involves storage and retrieval of information. Memory can be short term or long term and both of these are influenced by stress. All information is first stored in short term memory (available for immediate recall) and then depending on the 'instructions' or intention of the person the selected items are stored in long term memory. Results of researches in the area suggest that the items that cause low stress are stored better in short term memory and are therefore recalled immediately after they are received, but are forgotten soon after. The situation is different with items of high stress value. Such items are not only remembered longer but there is also some reminiscence about them and off and on they flash upon us and we tend to review them. These reminiscences affect our functioning as they interfere with our concentration on other tasks. An illustration will help to understand the phenomenon better. A person going on a long journey finds his journey full of events, some of which are highly stressful like harassment by the ticket checker or some lost luggage. After some time though the person may not be able to recall the minor and ordinary events but he well remembers the harassment and the losses he suffered, often imagining the various ways he could have handled the situation in a better way. Such reminiscences are common after experiences of severe stress such as some disaster causing severe trauma. They may even linger on in a pathological way causing what is known as post traumatic disorder.

Another effect of stress on memory found under experimental situations is that though items are recalled but they do not appear in clusters as they otherwise do under low stress situations. The recall is haphazard and incoherent, like in the case of an accident when, though, one can recall different aspects of the situation, but may not be able to put them together into a coherent picture of interrelated events. This is because only those aspects of the situations are remembered which have greater impact on the person. A good evidence of such 'distortion of memory' is found in the reports of witnesses of a crime or an accident where descriptions seem to be highly distorted and confusing. Both the victims and the observers are generally able to recall the act but often fail to recall the weapon of crime or the face of the criminal.

Stress Brings about Cognitive Shift

While responding to any event, we look for coherence in relationships among events within a situation. Most important of these relationships is between the person and the stressful event. In a stressful situation the questions to which a person seeks an answer are, "Can I control the situation?" "Can I cope with it?", "Who will be responsible for my success or failure in handling the situation?" In trying to handle a stressful situation one tries to answer these questions so that there is minimization of stress. An important way in which stress is handled is cognitive shift. The changes in the meaning of the situations, in other words, the cognitive shift can take a variety of forms. One such shift is called 'attribution process'. Attribution is the process of ascribing situational characteristics to the person. While perceiving a situation we get direct messages from the situation and give them meaning on the basis of our experience and knowledge about the situation. In social situations the cues available are used to interpret the behaviour of others and we ascribe certain characteristics to the people. This ascribing of the characteristics is attribution. These attributions are often temporary and situation specific, e.g. you make a bet and win and attribute your victory to your intelligence or to God's grace. In other situations the attributions can become permanent and get generalised and take the form of Locus of Control that explains a person's thinking about control of the outcome of any effort at managing things. Locus of Control within a person becomes evident when a person starts feeling that all the good or bad things in his life are because of a particular agent like 'wearing of a charm', 'parental guidance' or 'his single handed effort'. When responsibility for the consequences of an action is attributed to luck, chance or powerful others, it protects against self blame and guilt, both of which are powerful stressors. In an experimental study it was found that in patients going in for major surgery the 'Locus of Control' is shifted towards externality and the surgeon is perceived as an all powerful person, but after the surgery Locus of Control shifts toward internality. The successful recovery from the surgical operation helps the patient to regain the sense of control.

An important form of attribution involves ascribing situational characteristics to other persons rather than to situation or to problem causing stress. In many a social situation the source of stress is attributed to persons and situations other than the actual source of stress. In-laws and other relatives are often blamed for marital conflict and incompatibility instead of the marriage partners where the actual problem may exist. There can be many more such examples where one group may put the blame on other group or persons for problems in which they may not have a role to play. It is these attributions that become the bases of social prejudices and inter-group hostility.

Stress-related Cognitive Shifts, Attributions and Self-image

A closely related phenomenon of cognitive shift is a shift in the self image. Under conditions of prolonged stress there is a shift in cognition not only about the situation but also about one's own self. The shift in cognitions depends on the experiences of the person. Success in managing a stressful situation brings a shift in cognition different from that in case of a failure because these experiences interact with the attribution one makes about the experience of success or failure.

To provide coherence the experience of success or failure has to be attributed to some agent. When a person attributes the experience of success to himself, it enhances his self-image but if he attributes it to another external agent, it lowers his self-image. With experience of failure the effect is likely to be opposite. Attribution of failure to self lowers the self-image but its attribution to an outside source helps protect the self-image. When an aspirant for a job despite his high qualifications, brilliant career and satisfactory performance in the interviews fails to find his name among the selected candidates, he asks why? Why did it so happen? Where did the things go wrong? And, in his attempt to find an answer he may either attribute his failure to some of his own shortcomings like lack of right contacts or to the circumstances of the situation like better candidates and their performance or the bias of the interviewer etc. Both types of attributions are likely to have different impact on the self-image. Self attribution for the failure lowers the self-image while attribution to others protects against self blame by keeping the self-image intact. The significant thing is that these attributions may not match with reality and simply be a case of cognitive distortion.

Stress Interferes with Decision-making Capacity

The cognitive effects of stress i.e. narrowing down of attention, incoherent recall of information and cognitive shifts — all of these processes are likely to interfere with rational thinking and decision-making ability of a person. Since the internal changes taking place during stress call for attention, the attention from other important aspects of the problems gets drifted and as a result many a times people take important but incorrect decisions under conditions of stress like during illness or when they are emotionally exhausted. Eric Cassell from his studies on sick people has shown that during illness people lose perspective on the situation. He reports that people when ill are not able to solve reasoning problems that a child can easily solve. Normund Wong, a psychiatrist at California University admitted that after a major operation he totally lost perspective of the things and told worker colleagues that he would be at his work even when he had been told that he wouldn't be able to go for work for six months. It so happens because under stress cognitions are based on limited information and facts get distorted and decisions based on these distorted facts are not likely to be productive.

Stress Affects the Performance

The relation of stress with work performance is complex. This is so because many variables like motivation, style of working and effort etc., intervene the influence of stress on performance. Stress causes adverse cognitive, emotional and motor effects that lower one's performance effectiveness. If sometimes the decrement in performance in actual work situation is not evident it is because it is camouflaged by increased efforts and motivation one puts in to counteract the stress. The fact that stress lowers performance effectiveness is well demonstrated in experimental studies. The effect of stress on work is seen either in decreased output, fall in quality, increase in cost through wastage of material or in increased effort. Sometimes performance in one aspect of work may though remain constant but the cost rises in another aspect of performance. In a study when students were made to write a composition under stress, it was found that though they could maintain their speed but the sentences they wrote were short and the vocabulary they used was also narrow.

Field studies show that noise and overcrowding have very deleterious effect on performance. Children brought up in crowded homes are found to show deterioration in their school performance. A similar effect is observed in children brought up in noisy surroundings and in overcrowded classrooms. However the effect of overcrowding on performances depends upon a situation being appraised as crowded. If in a crowded classroom there are pleasant interactions, the classroom may not be perceived overcrowded. Consequently, it is not likely to greatly affect children's performance. The adverse effect of crowding also depends on the role people play. If everyone present is able to contribute something that is meaningful to others, stress through overcrowding is not evident in people's functioning.

Like environmental stressors, internal states also interfere with performance specially if these states happen to be emotional states, like worry, anger or agitation. These emotional states are accompanied by certain inner sensations for example, a sinking heart, tense muscles or drying of the mouth. These sensations force the attention to be diverted from the task at hand and demand action like one looks for water when there is dryness in the mouth.

Cost of Maintaining High Performance

In the preceding paragraphs we have talked about deterioration in performance under stress. Deterioration in performance however does not always take place. Often people can maintain their performance level but not without some side effect and cost of some sort. Frankenhauser has shown that individuals under stress when trying to maintain their performance level incur increased cost both at psychological and physiological level. The subjective cost is in terms of increased effort and higher alertness. At physiological level it is in terms of increased secretion of adrenaline, noradrenaline and cortisol. Experiments of Frankenheauser show that subjects exposed to white noise of high and low intensity, like that of a desert cooler or a computer, can maintain their performance at a higher noise level while doing an arithmetic problem; but there is a greater arousal in terms of increased adrenaline, noradrenaline and cortisol secretion, and increased heart rate. These indices showed as much as 120% rise in various parameters, which shows that the system is working hard to maintain the performance level.

Effect of Stress on Emotional Reactions

Emotional reactions are normally a part of stress response. When a person has gone through a prolonged period of stress, he continues to experience unpleasant emotions even when the situation is over. In day-to-day life it may not be directly evident because people refuse to admit them, as many social stakes may be involved in admitting that they are upset. For example, a child would not like to admit that his family is on the verge of break up. Similarly, a young man aspiring for a position for which there is cut-throat competition would not admit that he is worried or anxious though he is experiencing these emotions. The most common reactions to stress are anxiety, anger and agitation. When these emotions are not allowed to be expressed, a person may experience helplessness and depression. This depression, experts say, is not of psychiatric nature but has an origin in the realistic response to high stress reaction. Many job situations pose a very high risk to survival and therefore fear and anxiety are very natural reactions to such stressful jobs. Construction workers on high rise buildings, drivers of city transport, aeroplane pilots, astronauts and health workers working in units like titanus, AIDS or radiotherapy work under constant apprehension about risk to life. In other less stressful situations also similar reactions occur. A modern young woman, who, unlike her mother and aunt, has not been socialised to believe that her brothers deserve a special treatment, constantly lives a life full of resentment and discontent. Such emotional reactions are globally labelled as a feeling of distress. People working on simple monotonous job also constantly experience such distress.

When exposure to stress is prolonged and negative emotions have also remained aroused for a long time individuals stop reacting with emotions. They become cold, indifferent and detached and all these reactions have a detrimental effect on their social behaviour. How do these reactions affect a person's behaviour are reviewed in the following section.

Stress and Social Behaviour

Social behaviour of an individual is the expression of his basic psychological need for affiliation. One fallout of cognitive changes and negative emotions experienced because of stress is the damage to the social behaviour of a person that may even lead to estranged social relationships. Many problems like social insecurity, selfishness and aggressions can be traced back to prolonged stress.

When people are burdened with the efforts to cope with stress, they do not wish to add an extra burden to their load. As a result they avoid social interactions and withdrawal becomes their preferred mode of coping with stressful social situations. Such behaviour is observed to be common among people living in crowded dormitories. To begin with, withdrawal is used to avoid unwanted social interaction but gradually it becomes a part of their nature. These people begin to avoid eye contact and conversation with others and show lesser and lesser cohesive behaviour. In the process they get isolated losing all the benefits that could come through maintaining social relations. Just as one avoids being with other people to reduce his burden of maintaining social relations, people also avoid and isolate him when he is threatened by negative feelings and ideas about his own self. This is what happens with people who undergo severe trauma like loss of a child or rape. Such people are observed to suffer alone. Parents of the lost child or the victim of rape may condemn themselves for the event. For them social interactions carry the risk of revealing such negative feelings.

Another effect of stress is a rise in aggressive behaviors. Pent up emotions emanating from a stressful situation are often displaced on the other people through aggressive behaviour. Fights and verbal attacks are commonly observed phenomena when people are upset due to some reasons, e.g. hostilities are common among people when there is shortage of space or other resources. This fact is observed both in real life situations and laboratory situations. For example, case studies of battered children show that the lives of their parents are in some way burdened with various stressors like too many children too soon after marriage. Antisocial behaviours like street fights, destruction of public property and pilfering of petty things can be traced back to aggression arising out of stressful situations. Such aggression can also take the form of homicide and even suicide when people are very desperate. In work situations also pilferage is often traced back to resentments and hostilities.

When people are coping with stress, they get so engrossed in their problem that one cannot expect them to be very sensitive to the demands of social situation, leave alone trying to help others. Being busy with their own problems people fail to appreciate or even differentiate between the role different people are playing in a social situation. For example, instead of analysing the total context we may blame the local politician for the price rise or blame the nurse for the deteriorating condition of our relative. Highly stressed persons often fail to recognise the role they should be playing in a given situation. For example, at a tender age when a child needs support and encouragement, the parents instead of fulfilling this need of the child demand from the child to play the parenting role. Another example of a failure to recognise the role one is expected to play is when, during an interview for a job a candidate, instead of highlighting his qualities and assets starts talking of the personal problems he is facing.

Disinclination to take responsibility for social welfare or being insensitive to others' feelings and interests or failure to participate in community affairs are some other examples of the manifestation of the same phenomenon. Many thinkers seriously feel that the cold indifference of the modern man towards others is due to the exposure to the ruthlessness of the two World Wars, many smaller wars and to the constant exposure to internal and external hostilities. If victims of accidents are left unattended on the roads, and torture and cruelties both actual and imaginary are enjoyed as a means of entertainment rather than to initiate action against them are all a result of prolonged exposure to stress which are manifestations of failure to recognise one's normative role in society. Such behaviour is becoming almost a universal phenomenon in modern urban life. In brief, it can be concluded that the social after effects of stress are manifestations of changes in cognitions, emotions, and social sensitivity. How they are coped with is the subject of the next chapter.

CHAPTER 5

COPING WITH STRESS

In earlier chapters we have talked about meaning, sources and after effects of stress. In this chapter we will attempt to explain what efforts people make to overcome or reduce stress. Before going into the details of these efforts it will be appropriate to state that these efforts have been generally grouped under the term coping. The study of coping implies that humans are active, adaptive beings who when faced with stress make efforts so that stress does not cause any undue damage to them. We have seen that when stress is not coped well it has an adverse effect. It becomes imperative, therefore, that we have a proper understanding of coping, its meaning, the various ways of coping and the consequences of coping.

What is Coping

Coping can be described as the effort made by an individual to eliminate or master the stressful situation so that his physical and psychological survival is ensured. Coping efforts are a manifestation of an individual's struggle for existence. In other words, because prolonged stress has the potential to cause physical and psychological damage, coping efforts are directed towards saving oneself from such damages. An individual's coping efforts are so well integrated into the web of life that people may not be conscious of the fact that their efforts are serving a special function to help them survive. Overcoming obstacles, avoiding unpleasant encounters and dangerous situations or changing the meaning of these situations are some ways of coping with stressful situations. Whatever be the circumstances coping is invariably an attempt at manipulating a situation so that it can be managed within one's available resources.

Is Coping a Specific Form of Response?

Coping is not any specific form of response. In fact, any effort that makes a situation less demanding and manageable qualifies to be called coping. These efforts may not always be in the form of overt behaviour. For example, a person under stress may appear to an observer to be sitting idle while he is actually trying to mentally handle a situation. Fantasizing or talking to oneself are some such forms of coping that are carried on without being exposed to observation by others. Coping also occurs as active behaviour such as fighting, running away from a situation, crying or physically removing the source of the stress. Let us illustrate this with an example.

You are waiting for some one. You are worried about the delay in his arrival. You get apprehensive about his safety and whereabouts and, therefore, you are experiencing stress. Consequently, you start making efforts at coping. You tell yourself, "Perhaps his train is late", or "Maybe he is caught in a traffic jam". Self-talk like this, though not observable by others is a mode of coping since it aims at reducing stress. But when you start contacting the railway or the police, your coping becomes observable as the efforts made by you take the form of overt behavioural activity.

Coping Involves Adaptive Changes

A stressful situation is a problem situation that demands some viable solutions. These solutions involve bringing about changes either in one's own self or in the external circumstances so that the situation no more remains stressful. As it is already stated, adaptation may involve changing either oneself or the stressor situation. An example will help in explaining the differences in the two types of adaptive changes. Assaulting an adversary so that he is no more aggressive is an example of changing the external circumstances, whereas submitting meekly to the same adversary is an example of changing oneself. As both behaviours aim at reducing stress they deserve to be classed as coping.

Coping has two Goals

Whatever be the nature of coping, it aims at achieving two things. Firstly, it has to manage the stress response, specially the unpleasant emotions and thoughts. Secondly, it has to manage the stressor so that it is not allowed to cause stress. When we look at an individual under stress we find that he is either trying to deal with his internal state or the stressor or he may be simultaneously trying to manage both. As an illustration it can be pointed out that keeping the various physical stressors like heat, noise etc. within tolerable limits, or maintaining good interpersonal relationships are some ways of managing the stressor. On the other hand, playing soft music, praying, or even indulging in various kinds of escapist behaviours like drinking or watching movies are some ways of managing the stress response. Both these types of efforts keep arousal level at low level. In other words whatever be the mode of coping ultimately it must control stress.

Coping is not a one Time Effort

Under no circumstance is coping a one shot attack on stress. Rather it is a continuous process of evaluating a potential stressor and the resources available, choosing appropriate strategies (coping efforts), trying them out and re-evaluating the entire situation. If stress is not eliminated, the cycle is repeated. Sometimes this entire cycle may continue for an unlimited time because the stressor situation tends to persist. However, during each cycle a different strategy is tried out till an individual finds a response capable of eliminating or reducing stress to a tolerable limit.

In this way under any given stressful situation one makes a series of transactions till the best balance between the demands of the situation and the response to it is achieved. The process is further illustrated with the help of fig. 1.

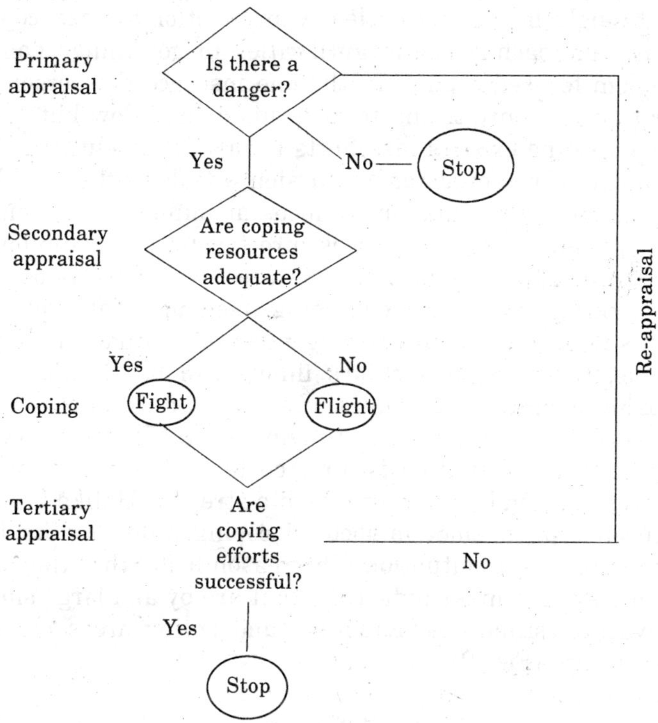

Fig. 1. A model depicting the coping process. Note that coping forms an integral part of stress. Coping continues so long as stress persists but takes the form of varied strategies with repeated cycles.

Coping Behaviour Differs in its Focus

As already emphasised coping has to negotiate both the stressor and the stress caused by it but at a given moment it has as its focus only one of them: either the emotions or the stressor situation. In the first instance it is termed 'emotion focused' coping and in the latter case it is the 'problem focused' coping. However, they are not two distinct forms of behaviours, i.e. the same behaviour may be in one case problem focused coping and in another case it can be emotion focused coping. When people very close to us are unwell we pray to God for their early recovery. This is problem focused coping but when prayers are offered for getting strength to go through the crisis it is clearly an 'emotion focused' coping. Again approaching some authorities to get things done is problem focused coping. In the one instance the person under stress is only trying to keep his anxiety low but in the other case he expects his efforts to provide a solution to his problems. The foregoing discussion should suffice to show that coping may differ in its focus at different occasions.

Problem focused coping is directed towards elimination or reducing the potential of a situation to cause any damage or harm. Problem focused coping itself may take different forms depending upon the exigencies of a situation. For example, threat from a child's illness can be eliminated by seeking medical help while threat from an examination can be handled only through studying hard. Emotion focused coping in any situation is directed towards eliminating the distress caused by the presence of a stressor. Unlike problem focused coping, emotion focused coping differs in its form from situation to situation. The reason being that they have to manage the inner upheavals that are by and large similar in various situations. Laughing and crying are some such behaviours (Fig. 2)

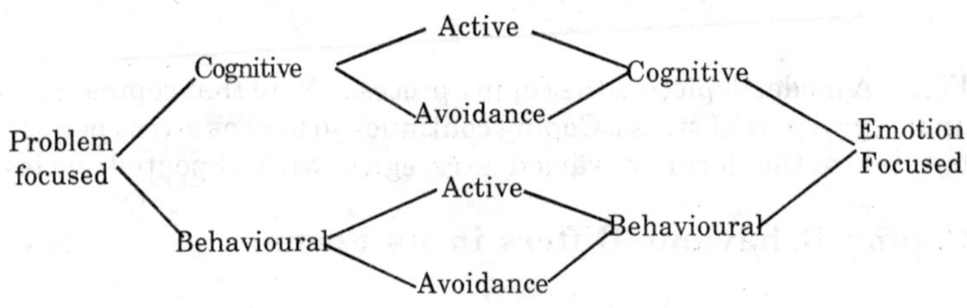

Fig. 2. A three way classification of coping

It is important to recognise here that the two functions may be served by the same form of behaviour or the same mode of coping may serve different functions at different times or for different people. For example, crying may be used for attracting attention and getting help or on other occasions it may serve as a means of relieving emotional tension. An analysis of the researches on coping suggests that the various forms of behaviour identified as the modes of coping can be grouped into five broad categories. These are (i) information seeking, (ii) direct action, (iii) inhibition of action, (iv) turning to others and (v) utilising intra-psychic processes. A brief explanation of these five modes will help in getting an understanding about such forms of coping.

Information seeking as a way of coping involves efforts to know more about the situation and the possible solutions to the problems that are causing stress. Reading books and magazines, consulting experienced people or holding discussions or even carrying out investigations, i.e. acting as one's own detective, are some ways people adopt to gather information.

Direct action is a more practical way of coping with stress. It implies taking concrete steps to remove or reduce threat. Activities like snubbing an offending colleague, getting an illness treated, changing jobs or the working environment and studying for an examination are all examples of direct action. In any single situation direct action can take a variety of forms. For example, a man pestered by hunger may either prepare food, beg for it, buy it or snatch it from some one.

Contrary to direct action is the inhibition of action, i.e. under severe stress a person may stop doing any thing, which may not be an outcome of any deliberate decision. Dazed inactivity is typical reaction to a severe trauma. Inhibition of action includes all attempts at tolerating the stressful situation specially when there is no apparent solution to a problem. For example, in case of a terminal illness of a dear one, waiting and watching is the only way of coping. Inhibition of action is evident most naturally in the 'freezing' behaviour of animals. When animals are cornered by a predator, they simply freeze and become motionless so that they appear dead and are, therefore, left alone.

The fourth mode of coping identified is turning to others for support and help. Value of support seeking and being with others is discovered very early in life. An infant's clinging behaviour, its 'cry' to call the mother are the beginnings of support seeking behaviour. Support seeking or turning to others as a form of coping is so important that a separate chapter has been devoted to it (Chapter 10).

The four modes of coping discussed so far occur as overt behaviour. However the fifth form of coping is intra-psychic coping where the coping takes place at the cognitive level and, therefore, cannot be observed by others. These processes include all the cognitive activities carried out for controlling or managing stress. Analysing a problem, redefining and reevaluating it or giving self-assurance or self-instruction are all important forms of coping. Fantasizing is another commonly used intra-psychic coping. It is an effective manager of stress to obtain a short term respite from it. Fantasy is one among the many coping strategies that is not bound by the demands of reality. No one stops us from killing our adversaries or becoming big bosses in fantasy. Fantasy and many other intra-psychic forms of activities help in safeguarding against painful emotions. Coping, which is used only to protect oneself from the painful emotions, is known as defensive coping. Sigmund Freud introduced the concept of defence mechanism to explain the intra-psychic coping that goes on involuntarily to protect oneself from the painful emotions likely to cause stress. Use of defence mechanisms make the situation more tolerable even without actually removing the stressor. As psychological processes they are not different from any other cognitive process, only they have a very specific purpose. For example, logical analysis is a basic cognitive process. It can be used as a normal coping or can be used as a defence mechanism of rationalization. Under normal circumstances any adult may show childlike frivolousness. But as a defence it takes the form of regression when an adult behaves childishly to escape a situation.

Temporal Dimensions of Coping

When it is said that coping involves a series of transactions it implies that coping occurs over a period of time. Every transaction is followed by an evaluation and necessary modifications in the response. How long such an activity continues and what are its timings in relation to it depends on the nature of the stressor, individual's perspective about the stressful situation, and the pervasiveness of the impact a stressor makes. The interplay of these factors has three implications.

1. Coping adopted by an individual can be a long-term solution to a problem or a short cut to stress management. Feigning illness to escape an examination is a short-term solution to a problem while preparing oneself for it through regular studies is a long term solution to the problem.
2. Coping effort itself can differ in its duration. In an emergency coping can be sudden and drastic. In other situations where stressor is persistent and is causing chronic stress, coping too can be persistent. Living in a noisy or overcrowded home or working in a low status, low satisfaction job are some examples of situations that generate chronic stress and demand persistent coping.
3. Another temporal dimension of coping concerns the timing of its occurrence. Normally, coping is assumed to be a part of the stress process and takes place when stress occurs. But coping can also take place before the occurrence of a stressor event (anticipatory coping). When a stressor event is predictable people can get ready for them. Rehearsing for an interview, or equipping oneself for a future event are well-known forms of anticipatory coping. Anticipatory coping with the death of a terminally ill person occurs as crying. Analysing the consequences of a death in the family is an attempt at coping with impending death. As the condition deteriorates people start talking and behaving as if he does not exist. This type of behaviour is also an attempt at coming to terms with the impending loss of a person through anticipating a coming event. Coping can also occur after the stressor event is over (post-stress coping), like talking about an event that has gone by, describing it to others or fantasizing how one could have dealt with that situation for a long time after the trauma is over. Crying, mourning and reminiscence are some common forms of post-stress coping. All such behaviours are attempts to overcome the residual effects of stress.

The Choice of Coping

The five modes of coping described above are broad groupings of coping strategies from which an individual chooses the ones he considers most appropriate in a given situation. He may be shifting from one strategy to another, from moment to moment or may be using more than one strategy at a given moment (e.g. crying and running away from a danger). Coping is a complex behaviour that is not easy to describe. It is equally difficult to explain how a person decides what coping to use when. An attempt is made here to explain how a choice is made about the coping to be adopted. This will help in appreciating that the choice of coping is not made in a haphazard way and that people approach a problem in a very systematic way. This choice generally depends upon an interaction between the situation- and person-related factors. Among the person related factors the most important are related to appraisal of the situation and one's own resources. For example, if resources are judged as adequate and a situation is appraised as a challenge more 'problem focused' coping occurs. Here, the coper feels confident about the possibility of solving the problem (i.e. removing or reducing a stressor). In a situation of challenge, there is no distress, therefore, more objective evaluation and selection of strategies is possible. Conversely, when resources are adjudged as inadequate there is a high degree of threat leading to high emotional arousal. Because of high distress coping becomes emotion focused and denial and avoidance become preferred modes of coping. These forms of coping can at best reduce distress but provide no help in removing the stressor. Workers in high stress occupations like in construction work often act as if the job has no danger or threat. When an accident occurs it is the worker and not the job that is blamed for it. Similarly, often individuals suffering from some serious illness use denial and behave as if there is nothing wrong with them. They may even avoid social interaction so that their illness, pain and misery are not realised by others.

But there are other sets of problems in which the demands of reality are so concrete that they cannot be denied or avoided. In such situations coping by different people tends to be more or less similar. These situations have come to be known as life events and include happenings like birth of a child, death of a dear one, marriage, loss of job or property etc. Most common reactions of people in such situations are denial and anger followed by acceptance. Only with acceptance does the problem-focused coping begin. In these situations denial may be sometimes so prolonged that the situation may go out of control. Delay in seeking treatment of a serious illness is a typical example of such interrelationship between denial and delay in adopting problem-focused coping. There are also some problem situations where emotion-focused coping has no place. The threat posed by them must be attended through problem-focused coping. These situations concern the demands of day-to-day living, child rearing, housekeeping, earning a livelihood or maintaining the family integrity. However, within this set of problems every situation may demand a separate strategy. For example, in a family setting, while handling children people often use punishment, but for handling a marriage partner they might use negotiation (I will make tea while you make the beds).

In all types of situations there is one mode of coping which is universally used, i.e. turning to others. When people seek others' help, it is primarily in search of advice and information that will help in changing the stress causing situation.

In circumstances where the stressor situation cannot be changed, coping becomes intra-psychic. While coping at this level, an individual either tries to change the meaning of the situation or to distract himself from it. Strategies commonly used are "positive comparison", selective ignoring and fantasizing. Through positive comparison one tries to inject some positive valuation into the stressor situation, like "We are better off than many" or things could have been worse. For example, after a disaster people are thankful for having survived. This helps them to tolerate the loss of their belongings. 'Selective ignoring' involves avoiding to pay attention to a persistent cause of irritation, e.g. trying hard to concentrate on work and to ignore the unpleasant behaviour of the supervisor. In home situation children may absorb themselves in reading and television watching as a method of overcoming family stress. To sum up, people faced with stress go on adjusting their coping to achieve a balance between the demands of the situation and their own resources.

Outcome of Coping

The theme of this chapter so far has been that coping process is intricately woven into the web of life, preventing or managing stress. But what comes out of this constant coping has a long term implication depending on the extent to which it succeeds or fails in managing stress. Researches in the field of stress have repeatedly demonstrated that it is not stress *per se* but the way it is handled that affects people. When stress is successfully mastered, it has a beneficial effect of far reaching consequences. One emerges wiser out of a crisis if it has been handled effectively. Survival after a trauma like air crash, prolonged captivity, viz. prisoner of war or serious illness helps an individual to see life from a more mature perspective. Skills developed while coping with a situation become a part of an individual's resource repertoire and come handy in future. The most important skill developed while coping with stress is 'learning how to learn' new coping skills and strategies. Experimental studies have shown that even when people handle stressful situations under artificial conditions, effective skills are developed and used in real life situations.

But, when coping efforts fail they have adverse effects of serious nature. These adverse effects are directly related to the duration for which coping persists. If coping has to continue for long there is hardly any time to recoup the energy that gets constantly depleted. When energy level is low, the resistance to various illnesses also gets lowered and the person may easily catch various infections. Low energy level due to continued or repeated unsuccessful attempts at mastering the adverse physical and psychological consequences of stress sets in a state of helplessness in the person. Gradually it becomes ingrained in their response repertoire in the form of a trait known as learned helplessness These people might believe that no efforts of theirs will help in changing the life circumstances. As a result they stop trying. The trait of learned helplessness is most commonly observed in children, older people and in most women.

Maladaptive and Dangerous Coping

Besides the success and failure, the outcome of coping is decided by the extent to which the alternative behaviour opted for coping with a stressor event are adaptive or maladaptive. Adaptive coping helps in adjustment but sometimes under desperation or social pressures, people often opt for coping which may damage their health and well-being or make them socially misfit.

Addictions to various harmful substances give temporary respite from various stresses but these have a damaging effect on the general health and well-being. Sometimes people while not ingesting harmful substance may develop a tendency for overeating when stressed. An individual with such tendencies may be worried about overweight and other harmful effects of overeating but may not resist it because he does not recognise that it is a way of coping with stress. The opposite may also occur. A person may starve oneself till he/she gets weak and anaemic.

A yet another dangerous and maladaptive coping takes the form of 'hospital addiction'. The condition has been known in medical science as Munchhausen's Syndrome and as Fictitious Disorder. The sufferer, usually women in the age group of 30–40 or men in the age group of 40–50, tell exaggerated tales about their symptoms, get admitted in a hospital and enjoy their stay there. Sometimes they even cause injury to themselves. Painful investigations, starvations, intravenous drips and even operations are tolerated to escape from the demands of life for sometime. An equally maladaptive coping is manifested as delinquent behaviour like indulging in irresponsible sexual behaviour and high risk behaviours and exposing oneself to dangers of rash driving. These are ways of expressing resentment and dissatisfaction against an established order, specially parents and parent surrogates. Delinquent behaviours can only lead to jail terms and further decline in socially acceptable behaviour. At every stage such behaviours add to the existing stress rather than reducing it.

Effective Coping

The discussion about coping so far has concentrated on the cut and dry facts of theoretical interest. But the entire exercise remains incomplete without deciding as to what makes coping effective and how far anyone can make oneself an effective coper. Since stress occurs in a situation where an individual is trying to meet an environmental demand or to meet the internal demands within the limitations of the environment, effective coping must suit both the person and the environment. For example, a person who has suffered a huge loss in business must cope with it so that his efforts help him to attain a sense of well-being without jeopardizing overall adjustment in other areas of life. At the same time his coping must be in harmony with his values and beliefs. All this is a difficult task and, therefore, invariably requires some sort of compromise.

It must, therefore, be clear that coping may not always be effective. One reason for this as stated above is that one may not be able to fulfill all the demands of the situation, e.g. if a man has to pay a bribe for getting a job done and if this is against his value system his guilt will persist for a long time.

Another reason why coping is not effective, could be that it is not well thought out and planned. Under high stress when there is neither time nor mental state to think out a well-planned strategy, a situation has to be tackled through habitual modes. In such situations coping skills that a person has already developed come handy, and such habitual modes may help in meeting the threat from the demands of the immediate situation. But, if the coping adapted jeopardise the long term goals, coping cannot be considered effective. For example, if a young man assaults someone to cope with the humiliation caused, he may settle the score with this person but then later find himself behind bars. Often failure of coping can be ascribed to carry over of coping strategy from one situation to another. Since situations differ in their adjustive demands successful coping in one situation may prove disastrous in other situation. For example, acting helpless may be helpful at home where it brings about help and sympathy, but in job situations it would bring only disapproval.

The above discussion makes it clear that coping effectiveness is difficult to define. It cannot be given as a single one-sentence statement formula. Sometimes the demands of a situation are so complex as in social situations where the stimuli are ambiguous and subtle or complex that they put multiple demands where fulfilment of one demand is at the cost of another. In situations like this, perfect coping remains an illusive ideal. Still, certain broad generalizations about coping effectiveness can be made.

1. There is no mode of coping which is universally effective since different types of problems require different types of coping. When problems originate in the immediate environment, problem-solving efforts to eliminate the stressor can be effective, but when they originate in larger system, problem solving efforts of a single individual may not work. In these situations effective coping aims at reducing the emotional arousal only. This explains why people in the lowest rung of social system or in the job hierarchy become passive. For them use of alcohol or some such behaviour becomes the norm rather than a deviant behaviour. In such situations where there is a possibility of escape, fantasy and day dreaming may help, but, where there is no possibility of a let out, living with the problem becomes the most effective way of coping. Accepting a marginal existence in society or the aches and pains of old-age are examples of such coping through acceptance.
2. The vast amount of research in the field points out that since different forms of coping are required in different situations, an optimal coping style would comprise of a combination of intra-psychic and behavioural coping with both having emotions as well as the problem as their focus. If the focus is on emotions only and the problems that are the root cause of unpleasant emotions are neglected, the problem may not only increase but also intensify. For example, withdrawal or denial immediately after a trauma although gives time to recover from the shock but ultimately one has to face the situation and actively seek solution to the problem. In most coping higher problem focused coping is associated with healthiness as it makes a direct attack on the problem. Higher

intra-psychic coping is however associated with depression even if the coping happens to be problem focused. Intra-psychic coping when adopted after taking an action adds to stress rather than reduce it. Brooding over a lost chance cannot be good for anyone. This is the reason why people are advised to reflect a lot before taking an action rather than after the action has been taken. Reflection and analysis of where the fault lies can prevent breaking up of marriage even if it happens to be on the verge of breaking. Here, it may be added that such reflective analysis should be followed by constructive action that is effective in solving the problem — in this case if one strategy does not succeed, one needs to try another strategy. Pearlin and Schoolar observe that people who use a variety of strategies to handle marital problems can overcome stress in this area. In case of academic stress also, students who use a number of problem focused strategies come out successful as compared to those who use primarily emotion focused strategies.

3. Effectiveness of a particular mode of coping differs with the severity of stress experienced. Support seeking, which is an important mode of coping serves a useful and productive purpose when stress is high and the individual requires assistance in coping, with emotions and with the problem. But, when stress is low, support seeking may divert attention from the problem as social interaction demands both time and energy and support seeking is not possible without the concomitant social interaction. Similarly, giving up problem solving efforts may be the most effective way of behaving when problems do not have a realistic solution — an incurable disease or a problem that is not amenable to solution fall in this category of situations. Going into a hysterical trance or developing other psychological symptoms can also serve some useful purpose in overcoming the drudgery in life. But, if these happen to be the only mode of coping with every aspect and problem of life, they lose their effectiveness as a coping mode.
4. A rich repertoire of coping modes and adoption of a flexible approach in the use of these modes is the most effective way to cope with the stressors in life.

CHAPTER 6

STRESS AND HEALTH

Popular writings on stress start with the assertion that stress is a signal to danger. It is often called the 'hidden adversary'. Medical practitioners often hear their patients say that their malady occurred after some major stressful events which proved to be 'the last straw'. 'I had my first heart attack after I lost in business' or 'I developed breast cancer after I discovered that my husband had another woman in his life.'

If stress has a role in damaging the health of a person it must be understood properly for stress is one factor which can be controlled to one's advantage. But before talking about controlling stress, its relationship with health needs to be clarified. It is true that modern life is fraught with stress and many people are finding it difficult to cope with so many stressors. It is also true that mortality and morbidity, due to non-infectious diseases is increasing and stress undoubtedly plays an important role in it. But this does not mean that stress invariably leads to illness. Somc stress is essential for life.

The Good and the Bad Stress

Stress is an essential part of life. Experts like Hans Selye equate stress with life and its absence with death itself. Even if we do not agree with such an extreme view we know that the stress has a positive value in life. There are innumerable occasions when stress leads to an improved sense of well-being. We may call it 'good stress'. We can differentiate between the good stress and the bad stress. So long as a person can successfully handle a situation it leads to good stress. When stress provides 'opportunities' to try out new solutions to life's problems and leads to new insights which are useful in future it is good stress. It is also good stress when successful handling of a situation is ego-boosting. Such stress is experienced in situations which are apparently beyond one's control.

Situations which can be easily handled do not cause stress, situations which are somewhat difficult, need some extra effort, but do not upset a person's functioning, cause 'good stress' since they provide a challenge. But situations which are uncontrollable and unpredictable and cannot be handled easily even with an all-out effort cause 'bad stress' since under such circumstances stress tends to persist.

Good stress is a 'must' for life. It acts as a motive force which helps people to explore, to grow and to test their own capacities. Even when the situation is highly stressful and people handle it well, they come out of it healthier, since they provide a sense of mastery. Such encounters with situations which cause good stress are frequent. Our lives are full of problems. In the normal course of life crises come, and are overcome, and individuals come out of these situations more mature and wiser. Such evidences prove that when a stressful situation is utilised as an 'opportunity' rather than as an occasion for self denigration and self pity, it causes good stress.

Good stress also occurs in situations which allow an 'other directed' meaningful action as it happens in times of disaster. In many community emergencies where people get mobilised for acting together to save others and take care of survivors are examples of 'good stress' situations. Many studies, show a decrease in crime rate and mental hospital admissions during such calamities.

Occasionally people convert bad stress into good stress by redefining a situation i.e., they perceive a positive meaning in a stressful situation. The best example for such transformation of bad stress into good stress can be obtained from the warfield, where soldiers who consider their injuries as 'good wounds' do not complain of pain. These soldiers see their wounds as an opportunity to get relieved from the active duty and to go home. As a result the signals of pain are not sent to the brain. Similarly, martyrs throughout history have accepted death bravely and walked to the gallows willingly simply because they saw a higher meaning and purpose in their sacrifice. We can cite many examples from every day life in support of this viz. taking care of a person with alzehmer's disease is considered to be a highly demanding job. But both men and women who take care of their spouses afflicted with this condition report an increased sense of well-being through caring for their life partners. Many a high risk jobs like manning the vital installation of one's country provide immense satisfaction on this account.

But stress is good upto a certain limit after which it becomes bad stress. It can cause damage to the health and well-being if stress goes beyond that limit. The negative consequences of stress may range from mild psychological distress symptoms to serious illness depending upon the severity of stress experienced. However, it must be said here that the impact of stress may range from increased well-being to serious illness depending on whether it is coped effectively or continues uncontrolled (Fig. 1). When stress continues

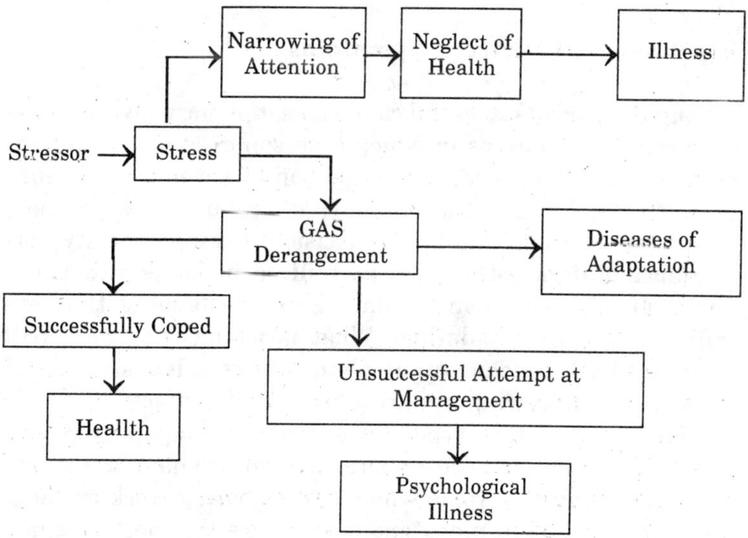

Fig. 1 A model relating stress and health

unabatted it can result in ill health — the extent and nature of which depend upon the presence of other factors, the most important among them are biological vulnerability and the environmental conditions under which an individual is going through a stressful experience. Levi has presented a beautiful model to explain how various factors interact to facilitate illness, the most important point expressed in the model is that stress is an essential factor but not sufficient in itself to cause illness. For example, stress is known to lead to hypertension. But in experimental situations when individuals are exposed to a high level of stress, only the susceptible persons show a rise in blood pressure. The fact that under the most difficult conditions everyone does not break down, shows that there have to be other conditions present to decide whether a person has mild health problem or a serious illness. In several disease conditions like cardio-vascular diseases or cancer, biological susceptibility is clearly established. In other conditions like depression, allergies or infections environmental factors are important. Without going into the details of the way other factors interact with stress, let us have an overview of the various forms of damage to health which are caused by stress.

Psychological Distress Symptoms

Among the various stressful conditions, the most severe stress is caused by situations in which a person does not have freedom. Such situations deprive a person of developing a sense of control. Because of various after effects of stress i.e., narrowing of attention and fall in decision making capacity performance suffers both in job as well as in home situations. Gradually the situation becomes so overwhelming that the individuals start wondering, 'What is wrong with me?' Self blame and self condemnation makes a person feel stupid and he starts withdrawing and avoiding social contacts.

Reactions of this type are common among people who function in circumstances where they do not have a 'control' over the situation. People who carry on boring work or those who are engaged in monotonous work are the most common victims of psychological distress. Working in these situations requires high alertness, so that individuals are not able to use fantasy or detract themselves away from the harsh reality. Machine based, dull and monotonous jobs commonly cause severe stress because of the above reasons. But other persons like managers and skilled workers also fall victim to it. So do the housewives who have to carry on the dull routine of household chores.

People with psychological distress react either with hyperactivity to avoid thinking about their own state or with a passive resignation e.g. watching television. Emotionally they are charged with irritability and other negative emotions which often get expressed in antisocial and aggressive acts like stealing, picking up fights, assault, homicide and suicide. If such emotionally charged state continues for long, they tend to go into depression because all the energy available is already exhausted. The state is termed as essential depression and often precedes any serious illness.

In modern times, with an increase in stress causing situations, the experience of distress is becoming a common phenomenon. Commenting on such a state Dejours writes in a W.H.O. report, 'Certainly it is demonstrated daily in clinical practice that tiredness, disappointment, deception, and sometimes 'ill' body resignation or on the contrary disturbing anger are apparent in conversation of patients who are not always being treated for depression.'

Psychological distress can often lead to adjustment problems of varying degrees. Studies in occupational health show that workers experiencing high job stress tend to develop resentments, irritability and other adjustment problems. Two of these manifestations are consumption disorders and burn out.

Smoking and Eating Disorders

These disorders are both symptoms of ill health as well as cause of various illnesses. Smoking is the most injurious form of behaviour. A variety of factors contribute towards initiation and maintenance of smoking. Tension, anxiety and work stress are among the most important contributing factors. People tend to increase smoking in the work place as their level of stress increases. Similar factors operate in other addictions. In the beginning they are used only as an experiment. When use of hard drugs shifts from experimental phase, associated with peer pressure, towards becoming a habit, social stress plays an important role. Persons who fall victim are in some way socially alienated and have a marginal status in the groups they belong to. They may find easy acceptance in marginal groups but pay the price through getting hooked to these drugs. Other consumption disorders emanating out of stress are concerned with excessive eating or selective eating of junk food leading to various deficiencies as well as obesity.

Use of Alcohol

Although there is not much evidence to prove that alcohol use takes place strictly in response to stress, people who tend to drink give stress as the reason for taking alcohol. Since use of alcohol is socially accepted and even eulogised, it is difficult for researchers to pinpoint the exact cause of alcoholism. However, there is evidence that people who resort to escapist drinking are usually alienated from their groups and have some anxiety related problems. In work place they are engaged in jobs, which are not given much recognition, are monotonous or boring. Chances of problem drinking increase if there is no social control i.e., no restrictions over drinking.

Use of alcohol is both a symptom of high stress as well as a cause of further adjustment related problems like, family fights, unemployment and social humiliations. Families of alcoholics are often ostracised. Financial difficulties force children to leave school and get involved in antisocial behaviour.

Burn Out

Human service jobs like teaching, social work and nursing put high demands for emotional investment. A stress related syndrome noted in persons belonging to these jobs has been recently identified and is given the name 'burn out'. Burn out results from a chronic emotional stress as persons in these professions often tend to have high expectations from themselves regarding 'others'. Sometimes these expectations tend to be bordering towards fantasy e.g., every patient must recover, every student must pass with high marks etc. As a result there is constant experience of failure and self condemnation. The feeling is not very different from the distress experienced in other professions, but is more intense.

The burn out syndrome is marked by specific physical, emotional and behavioural symptoms e.g.,

(a) Physical exhaustion
(b) Emotional exhaustion, low morale, over depersonalisation, and cynical attitude towards clients and co-workers.
(c) Behavioural symptoms comprising of lowered jobs accomplishment and lowered productivity.

Other symptoms which are often noted in burned out people are, cynical attitude towards the goals of the job one is doing, over self-confidence, frequent changes of jobs, escapist behaviour like use of sedatives and other drugs, absenteeism, withdrawal from others and physical illness. The occurrence of burn out is associated with an appraisal of work situation as highly stressful and unrewarding.

Post Traumatic Stress Disorder (PSD) — Reaction to Severe Trauma

Many drastic catastrophic events cause severe trauma and are reacted to with severe shock and disbelief. Since these events are sudden, people are not ready for them. Janis has recognised a three phase response in these situations i.e.,

1. *Anticipation* : The person gets aware of the impending nature of the events.
2. *Danger-impact* : There is an encounter with danger i.e., disaster, accident assult on any other such event. Usually there is a dazed state.
3. *Awareness of victimisation* : Once the danger is over, one gets aware of the losses and injuries to one's own self and to others.

Most individuals recover gradually from the trauma and start functioning as their normal selves. This recovery phase may be sometimes prolonged when an individual tries to come to terms with the event. But in some cases a drastic reaction occurs after the event is over. Because of its delayed appearance it has been given the name 'post traumatic stress disorder' (PSD). The disorder can occur in response to a natural disaster or a man made event like rape, abduction, riot, accident, etc.

The most common symptoms are avoidance and high arousal, for example.

(a) There are recurrent intrusive thoughts about the event, and desire to talk about the event repeatedly.
(b) There is a desire to avoid stimuli related with the event. A person may completely withdraw from social interaction e.g., a person who has witnessed an accident in job situation, may refuse to go to work.
(c) There is high arousal, high alertness and hyperactivity, and the person may try to do something just for the sake of doing something. In such a state he has difficulty in concentrating on anything and may experience recurrent nightmares and difficulty in going off to sleep. Lady Macbeth's somnabulism and Caesar's ghost as seen by Brutus are manifestations of PSD.

Now as the PSD is better understood it is being realised that the chief problem associated with the malady is the recurrent stereotyped anxiety bouts and dreams. Guilleminault and his colleagues have reported in the 179th Volume of The Journal of Nervous Mental Disease a case of delayed post-traumatic stress disorder. The patient developed extreme reactions seventeen years after she was repeatedly raped and tortured by three motor cyclists. She suffered from recurrent nightmares in which she relived through original experiences. During these dreams she developed sleep paralysis and upon waking up experienced dream like hallucinations. Her problems were so severe that she had to be treated with various drugs to sedate her and to relieve her of her anxiety. Hundreds of cases of PSD are treated after major wars. They are usually diagnosed as suffering from combat fatigue. Researches have shown that like other stress related disorders PSD is more likely to occur when people lose their feeling of having a control over the situation.

Stress and Psychosomatic Diseases

Since stress is a state of high physiological arousal there are wide-spread changes in the internal state during stress. When stress is short-lived the body states and the physiological systems come back to normal but if stress persists for long the altered body states demand attention and the individual under stress becomes painfully aware of them. The physiological changes are experienced as symptoms and are given the name of an illness. These symptoms can be varied and can be experienced in relation to any of the body systems. The possible symptoms related to various body parts are:

Muscular symptoms	: tension and pain
Gastrointestinal symptoms	: dyspepsia, indigestion, vomiting, heart burn, constipation and irritable colon
Cardiac symptoms	: palpitation, arhythmias and chest pain
Respiratory symptoms	: dyspnoea and hyperventilation
Central nervous system symptoms	: neurotic reactions, insomnia, weakness, faintness and some headaches
Genital symptoms	: dysmenorrhoea, frigidity and impotence

These symptoms are genuine experiences of a person undergoing stress. Since they are perceived as danger signals signifying some disease, the well-being of an individual is disturbed. The symptoms listed above though innocent in their own right can be a danger signal on several counts. (a) Firstly because they indicate that the individual is going through a very high level of stress. In fact they could be the body's 'cry for help' so that something can be done to reduce stress. (b) Secondly because the symptoms could be the first signs of some serious illness which occurs due to stress. The symptoms of many serious illnesses are similar to an exaggerated stress response e.g. chest pain could be the beginning of a heart attack, pain in the abdomen could be due to gastric or duodinal ulcers or the feeling of distress could be the first signs of gradually developing depression. In short the disturbed well-being due to stress could be in the form of some of the psychosomatic symptoms or could be a real full-blown somatic disease. Although stress is not the only reason for the loss of health and well-being and the presence of stress may not invariably lead to illness, stress does play a vital role in causing damage to a person's well-being, specially when a person fails to cope with it in an effective way.

The 'When' and 'How' of Stress-illness Relationship

The psychosomatic illnesses as discussed above form a major chunk of the conditions of disturbed well-being but there are other ways also in which stress can lead to illness. To begin with we can list at least three ways in which stress related behaviour can facilitate occurrence of illness.

1. Many serious events put drastic demands and the person has to make an all-out effort to cope with these demands. Happenings like bereavement, unemployment, migration, fall in this category. In case of such events coping has to be prolonged over several years. For example, the struggle of an unemployed person or the grief of parents of a lost child may reach the limits of an obsession so that danger signals coming from the body are neglected till the condition takes the form of full blown illness. Look at the following example — Rajbir has been a hardworking and honest worker throughout and has faced his opponents in a hostile job environment. A month before his retirement he starts putting all his records straight so that no one is able to point a finger towards him. He starts working long hours, feels exhausted but continues to pull on. A few days before his retirement he experiences heaviness in chest which he ignores considering it to be a sign of fatigue. During the farewell party, he develops severe angina followed by a massive heart attack.

   In this case Rajbir has ignored the inner signals of stress because he was too preoccupied with the events emerging out of his retirement. Had he listened to the inner signals, he could have taken timely action to prevent the calamity.

2. Secondly under stress not only are the inner signals but the simple rules of health also ignored. The most commonly neglected rules are also the most important ones. Nutrition, rest, activity and recreation are some of the commonly neglected rules of health. For example, a person may keep awake for long hours, take wrong food, become hyperactive or inactive—all these conditions are likely to facilitate disease conducive conditions within the body.
3. Thirdly people sometimes adopt modes of coping which are health damaging. Among these the most commonly used strategies that have been observed are use of alcohol and other drugs, smoking, reckless driving. In some rare cases many health damaging events may be brought about to cope with family problems. For example one may get involved in accidents or attempt para suicide in the hope of resolving family problems.

Besides the behavioural routes other most important route through which stress leads to illness is through bio-chemical changes which occur during the stress response in the form of General Adaptation Syndrome. Several hormones are secreted during stress to prepare the body for tackling the threat. Normally the response subsides without any adverse effect but under prolonged or severe stress all the energy is depleted, the stage of exhaustion is reached, and symptoms of alarm stage recur. In other words, the body reacts if a new stressor has appeared. But because the energy that is in reserve is already depleted the stage of exhaustion sets in. It is during this stage that illness occurs because the internal functioning goes topsy tervy. How this happens is shown in sequence through the following diagram.

Threat — Alarm — Resistance & Coping → Recovery / Exhaustion

The disturbances that occur during this stage are in the form of either excess or deficits of various hormones. In prolonged stress the disturbed functioning pattern and the system gets conditioned at that level so that the system either continues to function at that level or repeatedly gets into that form of functioning if similar conditions recur. When such disturbed functioning persists, it becomes capable of causing both functional disturbances as well as structural damages.

When several stressful events occur one after the other the activated state is not allowed to come back to normal and the disturbed condition continues with all its adverse effects on health. The vast research in the area suggests that stress has a role in either facilitating or precipitating illnesses like mental illness, gastric ulcers, hypertension, stroke, myo-cardial infarction, sudden cardiac death, influenza, pneumonia, diabetes, cancer and multiple sclerosis. New knowledge about various bio-chemical changes taking place is accumulating and this is helping in understanding how stress can create illness inducing conditions within the body systems.

What Happens inside Body during Stress

During stress, as soon as a threat is perceived brain sends signals to the systems to get ready to face the threat; i.e. to either fight or to escape to safety. Several chemicals are poured into the blood stream which carry these signals to the various organs and instruct them to act in a particular way. The most important among these chemicals are hormones released by the adrenal glands so named because they are attached to the kidneys.

Two groups of hormones called cortico-steroids and catecholamines are secreted by the adrenal medulla or the inner core. Catecholamines play an important role in mobilizing acute adaptive resources during any emergency while corticosteroids provide a more enduring support during stress. Bio-chemical analysis of urine collected while a person is undergoing stress shows presence of these hormones. But there is a slight difference in the chemical picture if the person is also disturbed. Studies by Marian Frankenaueser show that when a person is performing under stress adrenaline (a catecholamine) is always high, but if the person is also distressed there is cortisol (a cortico-steroid) also present in urine samples. Thus, two types of stress profiles emerge, stress with distress and stress without distress.

Experimental and other laboratory studies give evidence of the way the raised levels of these chemicals and their after effects in the form of other chemical changes are associated with various forms of pathology. For example, a high level of cortisol is associated with disturbances in immune system of the body. The importance of immune system in the body is similar to that of a protective army or police in a country. It guards against the various intruders like infections, allergies or any other foreign elements like tumor grafts. This is the reason why people develop allergies or infections while undergoing stress. In experimental situations animals who are given a graft of tumor tissue, when exposed to high stress, tend to develop tumors, the low stress animals on the other hand reject the tumor grafts.

High level of adrenaline is associated with raised levels of diastolic and systolic blood pressures. If stress persists high level of blood pressure also persists till the raised level becomes established and the person suffers from hypertension. The bio-chemical insights have helped in understanding the link between stress and illness. They have also provided a support for the theory that stress plays a part in causing illness.

Stress and Hypertension

Both animal and human studies show that subjects working in high stress situations tend to develop hypertension. Air traffic controllers who work in high stress situations develop hypertension and this relationship between stress and hypertension becomes more marked when other factors like increase in age are also operating. As age increases, the effect of stress becomes more evident.

Stress and Coronary Heart Disease

Coronary heart disease (CHD) is a condition in which blood supply to the heart muscles gets reduced due to hardening and thickening of the artery walls. The condition builds up slowly as fatty substances get deposited and is related to the life style and also to the biological factors of the persons. When the blockage is complete, there may be complete stoppage of blood supply to the heart resulting in the condition called myo-cardial infarction (MI) when severe pain is experienced in the form of angina pectoris.

Researches on stress and CHD relationship show that when stress is high there is an increase in the level of cholesterol due to free fatty acids released by the lever. Cholesterol thickens the blood which makes it difficult for the blood to move freely through the blood vessels specially the coronary arteries resulting in CHD. Enthusiastic researchers have tried to look for the relationship between job stress and CHD. To begin with they could not find a relationship between job stress and CHD. But careful analysis later showed that it is not the job requirement *per se* which is a predictor of stress but the perceived stressfulness of the job which determines the occurrence of CHD. If, despite high demands, a job is perceived to be a 'challenge' it is not health damaging. Perception of the job as highly stressful depends upon a combination of job demands and job satisfaction. A job situation which provides a sense of control is not perceived as highly stressful. The sense of control comes from the job being within one's coping ability combined with autonomy for freedom to make one's own decisions. The situation is a little different for women as they need to experience a sense of control in the home arena also. For them work overload depends upon the demands at the job as well as in the home. For example, the chances of women having CHD increases with increase in number of children.

To sum up stress from the job is an important factor in CHD specially if it does not provide a sense of control.

Stress and Immune System

Exposure to stress is known to affect immune competence or the ability to monitor, recognise fight and expel foreign intruders in the body. Immuno competence has been found to be decreased when individuals are exposed to stressors like examination, loneliness and overcrowding and such other situations when they are distressed. That is why people under stress become prone to allergies and infections. In a study it was found that individuals who worked with video display units and who were also having other problems with their job tended to develop allergic rashes: Growth of tumor is considered to be an indication of immuno competence. In experimental conditions graft of a tumor tissue given to an animal is rejected if the immune system is functioning properly but under condition of immuno-suppression the tumor graft is accepted and the growth of tumor takes place. Relay and his associates showed through a series of studies that when animals were exposed to various stresses, there was a rise in secretion of cortico-steroids alongwith immuno suppression. In these animals there was an acceptance of tumor graft and rapid growth in tumor. Under these circumstances there was also a steep rise in mortality rates specially among female mice.

Human studies also show a positive relation between immuno suppression and tumor growth i.e. cancer after life events like bereavement and separation from near ones. These instances are related to acute stress but the effect of chronic stress is different. When people are exposed to chronic stress there is increase in immuno competence through habituation.

Stress and Gastric Ulcers

Gastric ulcers are a very common form of ailment. It is caused by excessive secretion of stomach acids. These acids help in digestion, but when they are in excess specially with no food inside to digest, they damage the stomach walls. This type of excessive secretion of acids is associated with experiencing of stress in experimental and non-experimental situations. Such conditions are also associated with prolonged emotional activation which tend to get conditioned. Experimental studies with rats show that when they are exposed to continued stress ulcers tend to develop more in animals which make unsuccessful attempts at coping. Human studies also show that people with high emotionality and high stress are more prone to develop ulcers.

Summary

The various illnesses and health problems discussed above cover the areas where there is clinical and research evidence that their occurrence is associated with presence of stress. However, the relationship of stress and ill health is not direct and simple. Importance of factors like biological vulnerability and environmental hazards like allergens, pollutants and viruses cannot be ignored. Psychological factors like 'Sense of Control' and mastery vs lack of control and helplessness too cannot be ignored. People succumb to stress only when they feel that they have lost control over the situation. However all of these factors can lead to disease only through biological changes.

It is interesting to note that whereas researchers are satisfied with the evidence they get to show a positive relationship between stress and illness, clinicians are firm in their belief that stress can lead to illness only when it is not successfully coped with. Successful coping with stress invariably leads to health since it promotes a sense of mastery and wellbeing. In these situations it becomes "good stress'.

Future research is likely to concentrate more on the factors which help individuals to be stress tolerant. Researches also will have to identify the stress which is avoidable and preventable so that people can function at an optimal level.

CHAPTER 7

MEASUREMENT OF STRESS

In the scientific study of stress, its measurement has come to be of immense importance. A proper assessment of stress is important not only for understanding its nature but also for its proper management. Every other day we come across new stress management programmes but we do not know much about their efficacy which can be established only by obtaining a valid and reliable measure of stress. This is important for experts in all disciplines who are in some way concerned with the management of stress i.e. an ergonomist, an architect and experts in sports, medicine or industrial efficiency.

This chapter provides an overview of the variety of methods available for measuring stress. Some of these are simple and can be used by anyone, others are sophisticated and their use requires special equipment and expertise has to be developed in their use. The interested person can choose methods suited to his purpose, interest and professional background. However, since stress has both a physiological and a psychological dimension it is better to take into account both these aspects while assessing stress. Even if only one aspect or a limited aspect is measured it is always better to use a battery of tests. Firstly because of the complexity of stress phenomenon itself, secondly because the various measures do not always show a high correlation among themselves.

The chapter is by no means exhaustive in nature and gives only a broad perspective of the methods available at present. Measurement of psychological indicators of stress is given first. It is followed by a description of physiological measurements. The last section covers the non-intrusive or indirect methods. Some of the measures can be used only under laboratory conditions and cannot be used in real life situation. Others can be used for assessing stress under natural conditions. Some of the laboratory methods have been successfully adapted for field studies also and have provided an immense understanding about the stress phenomenon.

Psychological Stress Measurement

The measurement of psychological aspect of stress has been concerned with aspects such as cognitive, emotional, performance and behavioural. Some of these methods imply observational techniques in which a person functioning under stressful conditions is observed by the investigator. Others as you will notice, yield purely subjective data. The choice will depend entirely on the purpose for which measurement is being done. For example, if we wish to know the extent to which a certain working condition or the life circumstances which cause stress in a person, self-report methods become the choice, but if one wants to know whether a change in working conditions has increased or decreased stress, it is important to know the changes in the performance and observation has to be done. These differences will be clear after going through the following section.

Measurement of Cognitive States

As you can judge from your own experience, assessment of cognitive functioning requires both subjective as well as objective assessment techniques. A look at the techniques commonly used for this purpose will make this point clear.

Cognition has a number of parameters but since our purpose here is only to explain the techniques of measurement, description is limited to five parameters only. The parameters selected are (i) alertness, (ii) selectivity, (iii & iv) fast responding (which includes speed and accuracy) and (v) short-term memory. You will note that for each parameter a different set of devices is required.

Alertness: This refers to the subjective experience of arousal. At different times a person may experience different levels of arousal i.e. arousal after a certain amount of sleep-loss will differ from the arousal that is experienced after taking a few cups of coffee. The measuring device should help in assessing these differences. For this purpose a self rating is obtained on a simple rating scale or on a visual analogue. (See examples)

Example — 1

At present how alert do you feel? Please tick the remark which best describes your present alertness.

	Awake and very alert	Awake but not very alert	Feeling drowsy
You are	▱	▱	▱

Example — 2

Rate your alertness on the scale given below. Number 5 stands for very high alertness and number one stands for the lowest alertness i.e. drowsiness. Circle the number which you think is the best indicator of your present state.

1 2 3 4 5

My level of alertness

In a formal laboratory setting the subject can give response with the help of a paper and pencil. But in field observation when 'on the line' measurement is taken, the subject speaks out this response over a microphone and the response is recorded by the investigator or it is recorded by an automatic electronic device e.g. a tape recorder.

Selectivity : Selectivity is defined as the focusing of attention on certain task or activity or a setting. Selectivity is a basic requirement for carrying on any task except for a completely repetitive task. Since stress tends to decrease the ability to selectively focus attention on a particular task, the level of stress would be indicated in a decrease in performance. In a measurement situation the subject is required to carry on a simple task of identifying certain stimuli. Performance under stress is compared with the baseline performance of a subject and the decrease in performance is taken as an indicator of stress.

A commonly used situation to measure selectivity is Stroop test. This test comprises of a list of the names of various colours. These names are presented in a different colour than the colour name. For example blue is printed in red and red is printed in green etc. the task of the subject is to either read the words, or name the colours in which a word is printed. The speed of responding under normal conditions is compared with the responding against a background of an added stressor like noise. The difference in response rate is taken as an indication of fall in selectivity and therefore an index of stress.

Fast Responding : How fast an individual responds, without making an error, is a parameter of speed and accuracy both of which are measured together. When applied to measurement of stress, the method requires the subject to respond to a signal against the background of a stressor stimulus. For example, the subject may be required to respond to a buzzer by pressing a bar, or it could be a puzzle, to be solved. The stressor could be a state of competitiveness or fatigue or any other known stress causing stimulus. Comparison of speed of performance under stress is done with that in a non-stressful situation.

Short-term Memory (STM) : The assessment of STM involves presentation of some stimulus matter such as a list of words or numbers (under stressed and non-stressed situation), the subject is required to produce the matter in a given order. Measurement is done in terms of amount of matter correctly reproduced.

The methods of assessing cognitive states were devised originally for use in the laboratory situations but they have been used successfully in the field studies also. The most useful application is in the job situation and in clinical studies in medical settings.

Measurement of Emotional States

You will recall that emotional states are an important ingredient of a stress response. These states are measured mainly through subjective reports. Remember, emotional states are a condition of arousal which is interpreted as emotions by the person experiencing them. This is why the commonly used techniques rely on the subjective reports of the person experiencing them.

However in recent years, observational techniques also are being developed. Both these types are given here in brief.

Self-Report Methods

The most convenient way of knowing what emotions an individual is experiencing in a given situation, is to directly enquire from that individual. For example anyone going through a tough experience like prolonged isolation or food deprivation or standing on a precipice, is asked to describe the emotions he is experiencing. The description is then recorded by someone else. Recording is done either automatically or through the use of paper and pencil. These recordings can later on be analyzed by an expert.

Interview technique is also used for this purpose. An individual after going through a stressful situation is asked to describe the way he felt in a particular situation.

Standardised tests for assessing emotional states are also commercially available. These tests have a list of descriptive words or statements and the subject has to mark those which are applicable to him and those which are not. A few of these tests are listed below:

1. Spielberger's State-Trait Anxiety Scale
2. Spielberger's State-Trait Anger Scale
3. Buss-durkee Hostility Inventory

All the methods of measuring emotional states discussed above are self report methods in which assistance for recording is taken from others. Because of the fact that an emotionally aroused individual may not always be in a position to evaluate his internal states, attempts are being made to develop methods which would allow observation of emotional states.

Observational Methods

Recently some innovative methods have been tried out for assessing emotions through observation. The most effective among these, try to assess emotions on the basis of voice recordings. An individual while carrying on a task against the background of stress producing stimuli, is required to continuously speak. His speech is recorded on a tape recorder. Later on an estimation is made of emotional arousal through recorded voice. Observation can be used to estimate agitation, stupor or shock. Although these techniques provide objective information, they always pose the problem of validation i.e. observational records do not always tally with subjective reports. These facts have to be invariably taken into account when objective measurement of any subjective experience is taken.

Measurement of Behavioural Effects

Measurement of behavioural effects of stress is dealt with under three broad headings (a) Measurement of Behavioural Changes in Social Situation, (b) Measurement of Changes in Performance and (c) Measurement of Coping. The reason for choosing these parameters is that they have been found to be most conspicuously affected by stress.

Measurement of Behaviour Reactions to Stress under Social Situations

Assessment of behaviour under social situation is possible through observational techniques only. An individual is put either in a contrived or in a naturally occurring social situation, and exposed to some stressor. Observation has to be made in terms of occurrence or non-occurrence of certain specified behaviours. Through these items, answer to many questions can be sought e.g. 'Does he show socially positive behaviour?' 'Does he seek help?' 'Does he withdraw from others?' 'Does he offer help?' Behaviour is to be rated in terms of occurrence or non-occurrence of a behaviour. If many forms of behaviour are to be rated a checklist may be used. Sample items in a checklist are being given here as an example.

Sample Checklist Items

	Response Categories	
	Yes	No
Smiles	....	....
Seeks help	....	....
Withdraws	....	....
Offers help	....	....

Observation may be done either directly when the behaviour is occurring or otherwise a video recording may be done and behaviour analyzed later on. Care has to be taken that the camera is not visible to the subject.

Performance Measure

Although it is a well recognised fact that stress influences work, it has not been studied frequently. Measurement of performance can be done both under laboratory conditions and in actual working situations. While in field studies the natural occurring performance is studied, in laboratory a subject is given a specific task to perform. The commonly given tasks are anagrams, sentence completion or proof reading. The reason for using such simple tasks is to bring about certain standardisation in the performance studied.

A number of performance variables have been identified. These include, quality and quantity of output, errors in responding, misses, blocks (failures to initiate a response), adequacy of performance (the ratio of actual output to a predetermined quota, time taken to complete a given task).

These measures take into account both the process and the product of performance. However caution is required to interpret the stress and performance relationship because many factors indirectly influence the performance which is not directly related to stress. Among these are the strategies an individual uses to minimise the stress. For example quantity of production may be reduced or the speed slowed down to prevent stress rather than as a result of stress.

As in case of social behaviour, video recording can be done to analyze performance. Use of checklist in evaluation is recommended whenever more than one performance variable is under consideration.

Measurement of Coping

Coping is the most natural reaction of any individual to a stressful situation since he/she must manage the stress. Because of the fact that it occurs as a consequence of stress, it cannot be directly an indication of stress. But because coping is an integral part of the stress it is worth mentioning here, the methods most commonly used to measure coping.

The techniques adopted for the above purpose, attempt to determine the extent to which a particular form of coping is adopted by an individual in a given situation. Care has to be taken to decide in advance whether one wants to know the type of coping an individual usually adopts in that situation or one is interested only in knowing the coping adopted at one particular occasion. One must always remember that no one adopts the same coping in every situation. For example coping with a child's illness can never be the same as coping with a child's academic failure.

Two types of methods are commonly used in measurement of coping. These are self report methods and interview. Both these methods have their advantages and limitations. The problem with self report is that an individual is not always aware of the type of coping adopted. Still self report has been used effectively and the predictions based on self report come out to be quite reliable. In self report methods, rating has to be usually done against an already existing list of coping behaviour. Self report methods can yield much important information about the coping behaviour.

The other alternative available is interview. The coping interview has to be structured and asks what people do or are doing to cope with a specific situation and what they feel about it. Since interview is a social situation, the responses can be influenced by the nature of the situation or the perceptions about it. The interviewer overcomes this problem by using a pre-established criterion to interpret the response instead of taking them on their face value. Interview has been used effectively by many investigators. The problem with interview is that it is time consuming and many investigators may not be willing to spend that much time.

Both of these methods i.e., self report and interview have the option of tapping one dimension or several dimensions of coping. The choice depends upon the philosophy of the investigator and the purpose of investigation. For example one may ask "Does an individual use denial in a situation X?' or 'What coping methods does one use in situation X?' The answer to the second question obviously requires a multi-dimensional measure.

One important observation made in the context of measuring coping is that people do not use the same type of coping in all situations. This has necessitated that a specialised tool is required to measure coping in any given situation. This is the reason why investigators need to construct their own tools to suit the purpose of an investigation. A number of tools prepared in course of research studies can be taken as models for future work. (See box)

Some Commonly used Devices for Measuring Coping

Byrn's Repression-Sensitization Scale
Goldstein's Coping-Avoidance Sentence Completion test.
Joffe and Nadich's Coping-Defense Measure
Cohen Avoidance-Vigilance Interview
Ways of Coping Scale
Billing and Moose Scale

Measurement of Stress as Part of Daily Living

The recognition of the role of catastrophic events and day-to-day happenings has led to the development of a new approach to the measurement of stress. The approach involves identification, compilation and then scaling of the events or conditions which cause stress. The technique requires a scale on which the stress experienced by an individual is to be measured. Three types of stress measurement scales are currently in use i.e. (a) Life-event Stress Scales, (b) Measures of daily hassles, and (c) climate scales.

Life Event Scales

The origin of these scales is in the clinical observations of Holmes and Rahe. While going through the case histories of their patients, these experts observed that any major psychiatric illness is almost invariably preceded by some catastrophic events. These events demanded drastic readjustment in the lives of an individual and therefore were highly stressful.

After going through hundreds of case histories Holmes and Rahe collected a list of commonly reported events of this kind. Through a complex procedure they determined the scale value of these events in terms of their stressfulness.

An individual is asked to report on the events experienced during certain period of time eg. last one year. The stress score of an individual comprises of the sum total of stress scores for the events experienced by an individual. A number of scales have been developed on these lines. Some of them are commercially available also. There have been minor variations in the preparation of the scales but the scoring method is same for these scales. A simpler but equally useful method is to count the number of events experienced by an individual and take the same as a stress score for an individual. (See table in box)

Sample Items from Life Stress Scale with Mean Stress values

Items	Mean Stress Value
Losing some valuable article in theft	10.20
Being in contact with people having a very different way of living, character etc.	8.29
Being victim of social discrimination	7.96
Problem regarding dowry in daughter's marriage.	11.53
Death of a spouse*	17.01
Minor illness requiring** medical consultation	5.43

* Item with highest mean stress value
** Item with lowest mean stress value

(From Life Stress Scale: Srivastava, 1985)

Daily Hassles and Uplifts Scale

A related technique divised by Richard Lazarus is concerned with the measurement of daily hassles. The stress scale developed by him lists the minor hassles which can cause stress. These are the on-going stressors which need constant coping efforts. The measurement technique involves collection and listing of minor irritants likely to occur in an individual's life. The listing also includes the pleasant events that tend to happen in an individual's life. The argument is that pleasant events counteract the effect of daily hassles. For example a hassle like long travel by public transport may be counteracted by 'hot tea served' on arrival at the office.

Climate Scales

If one is interested in more chronic sort of stress he may go in for the scales concerned with the "climate" or the environment in a given setting. These settings may vary from the family group to the large organisation. Moose and Moose have developed scales to measure environment in a variety of situations — These scales measure climate in terms of three social aspects which characterise the social environments. These are: 'relationships', 'personal growth facilitation' and 'system maintenance'. The scales are standardised and are widely used in research. The climate of a family and a work place are of common interest to the investigator.

Non-intrusive Methods

Methods discussed upto this point need direct involvement of an individual whose stress level is being measured. The results of these measurements often get distorted because of the reactivity to the measuring device. For example an individual may put in extra effort to improve performance or give a more positive report about the climate because he is being 'selected' for the study. Investigators often get piqued by the observation that respondents often distort their responses according to their perception of the purpose for which measurement is taken. In order to overcome this problem, they have tried to adapt two established techniques for the purpose of measuring stress. These are discussed under Trace Measures and Content Analysis.

Trace Measures

Investigators have identified certain tell-tale signs of stress. For example people tend to increase smoking, drinking tea/coffee etc. A non-intrusive method would involve counting the number of cigarette butts or the used cups. In the job situation one possible trace measure can be sick leave or unauthorised rest periods. In medical settings, a patients' stress can be measured through demands for analgesics and sedatives.

Such trace measures require (i) identification of behaviour which is indicative of stress for a particular individual or individuals, (ii) criteria of that behaviour in a non-stress situation, (iii) comparison of behaviour under the stressed and non-stressed situation. When these three conditions are fulfilled trace measures can serve a useful purpose in assessing stress.

Content Analysis

The other non-intrusive method of studying stress is content analysis. As the name suggests content analysis involves an analysis of the contents of some form of communication. It can be letters, personal diaries, speeches or drawings all of which are already in existence. But one can also get some such products made. Some of the possibilities are essays, stories and poems. The response to some projective tests like T.A.T., Rorschach etc. can also be used for this purpose.

Being an indirect method it does not put a direct demand on the individual. From the point of view of measurement content analysis can be treated as a method of observation in which observation of the products of an individual is done instead of making a direct observation as conducted in an interview of the individual.

The method involves deciding upon (a) the product to be observed, (b) the indicators of stress, (c) numerical count of the indicators in the product.

With the availability of computer programmes content analysis is an easily manageable method.

Content Analysis of Archival Data : In a place of work as well as in a community certain records are available which can provide an indication of the level of stress experienced by an individual or a group. Most important among them are medical records. Incidence of stress related illnesses can give an insight into the stress level. Similarly in job situation records of absenteeism, accidents and illness over a time indicate the level of stress. Records of a plant, or departmental record can be compared with the general population and taken as a measure of stress.

Physiological Stress Measurements

The measures discussed above take into account only the psychological aspects of stress. However a complete picture of stress can emerge only when the psychological evaluations are supplemented with measurement of physiological indicators of stress. In this section an overview is given of the measurements which have been in practice to assess stress at physiological level. These will include measurement of cardiovascular functions, locomuscular functions, neurological functions, glandular and endocrine functions.

Cardiovascular Functions

These are the most commonly studied indicators of stress. Among these and also the simplest indicators of cardiovascular function are heart rate and pulse rate. Simple measurement of pulse rate is obtained by placing the fingers on the radial artery and counting the pulse-beat per minute. Heart rate is measured through electrocardiography (ECG or EKG). Electrodes are put on the arms and the legs of the subject (or on any other part of the body) and the recordings of the voltage produced by the contraction of the heart are obtained. Counting the spikes in the ECG recording, produced by ventricular contraction can give the heart rate. If heart rate of an individual has to be obtained for a longer period needle electrodes can be implanted. It is also possible to get ECG recordings when an individual is engaged in various types of activities. A portable tape recording device unit known as Holter Test is used for this purpose. The recording is later on translated in the form of a paper printout which can be interpreted either visually or with the help of an automatic interpreting device.

The other common and the most obvious cardiovascular indicator of stress is blood pressure. Blood pressure can be measured both directly and indirectly. Direct measurement of blood pressure involves insertion of a needle in the artery.

To avoid this procedure, an indirect measurement is preferred. Measurement is taken with the help of a device called Sphygmomanometer. The device has four essential components i.e. an inflatable cuff to be tied around the arm, a bulb to pump the air in the cuff, a measuring scale to indicate the pressure, and a releasing device to adjust the air pressure in the cuff. Four types of sphygmomanometers are available. These are described here.

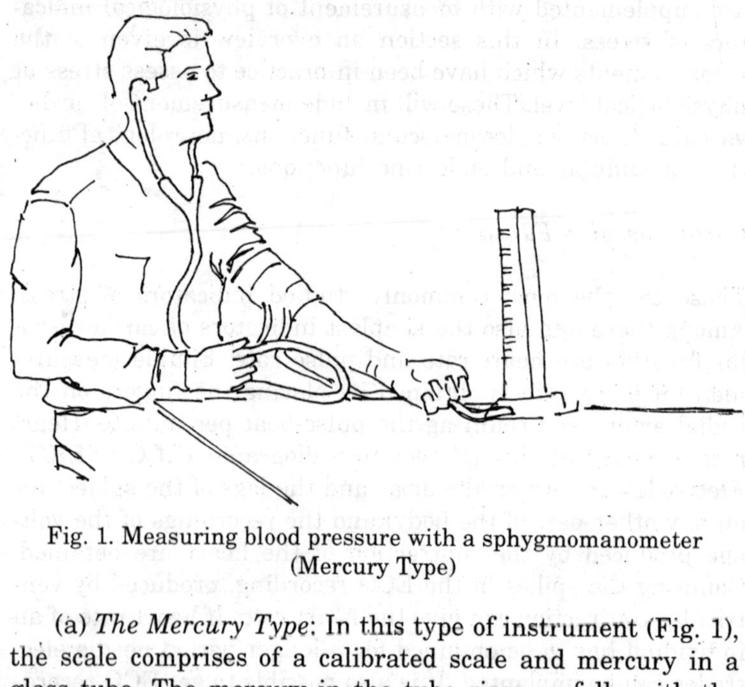

Fig. 1. Measuring blood pressure with a sphygmomanometer (Mercury Type)

(a) *The Mercury Type*: In this type of instrument (Fig. 1), the scale comprises of a calibrated scale and mercury in a glass tube. The mercury in the tube rises or falls with the increase or decrease of pressure on the cuff.

The measuring procedure requires that the cuff is tied round the arm, air is pumped in the bladder inside the cuff which increases pressure in the connected mercury tube making the mercury rise. When pressure is released mercury comes down. Palpation of the sounds in the brachial artery shows the changes in the pressure.

After tying the cuff, place the stethoscope over the artery, inflate the cuff to 33 mm height above the point where the sound of the pulse disappears. Slowly deflate the cuff and listen. The point at which sound appears is the systolic blood pressure. Continue releasing pressure. The point at which the sound again disappears gives the diastolic blood pressure.

(b) The Aneroid Sphygmomanometer: In aneroid instruments, the blood pressure is indicated on a clock type geared instrument with a pointer.

(c) The Modified Instruments: With advancements of technology semi-automatic and automatic instruments have been developed. They give digital readings of blood pressure. In that way they are easier to handle, but they are expensive and maintenance is difficult. Also they need to be constantly checked for reliability.

Locomuscular Functions

Many studies show rise in muscular tension with increasing stress. Muscular tension is measured with a technique known as electromyography (EMG) recording. Changes in muscular tension can be measured through a continuous EMG recording. The EMG is obtained from the whole muscle through electrodes attached to the skin.

Neurological Functioning

Since the brain is the central organ for regulating the response as well as the one responding to it the functioning of an organism is determined by the activation of the brain. Increase and decrease in activation as deviation from the optimal level is an indication of loss of efficiency which has been associated with stress. Low activity is associated with situations causing boredom. If the task is responsible one it is followed by panic and high activation. Such changes are observed through the electro encephalographic recordings (EEG). Specific wave patterns are associated with different levels of activation which can be subjected to observation and analysis through EEG recordings. EEG also like EMG involves recording of electrical activity.

Glandular Activity

Among all the duct glands the activity of sweat gland is most commonly studied. This is understandable since sweat glands increase their activity even under mild stress. Of the various methods developed for this purpose only two are being described here. These are colorometric method and the method of measuring skin resistance to electrical current.

For colorometric method a 25% solution of ferric chloride suspended in alcohol is applied to clean skin and allowed to dry. A piece of porous paper previously soaked in tannic acid and dried, is applied to the treated area. As the sweating occurs tannic acid reacts with ferric chloride. Amount of sweating is estimated by judging the colour of the strain.

The second method to be described here involves the estimation of skin conductance related with the activity of the sweat glands. The increase in sweating is associated with the lowering of the resistance of skin to the flow of electricity. Skin resistance is demonstrated to decrease with emotions. Because of this reason it is known as psychogalvanic response (EGR) or galvanic skin resistance (GSR). A weak electric current is applied to skin through two electrodes attached to the skin. This is connected to a device known as galvanometer. Readings on the galvanometer give an estimation of passage of electricity. Instead of galvanometer a polygraph can be attached to record the changes in the electric current. Evidence shows that under stress there is a marked change in skin resistance and makes it a useful method.

Endocrine Functions

Activity of the endocrine glands plays a crucial role in regulating the stress response. Researches during the last 50–60 years have clearly shown the role of the hormones. Among these the important ones are catacholamines produced by adrenal medulla and corticosteroids produced by adrenal cortex.

The techniques used for this purpose are loosely called biological assay. These techniques involve isolating a compound from a sample, purifying and then studying it. These are complex techniques and require a knowledge of bio-chemistry. The samples studied for estimating stress response are blood and urine. Repeated samples have to be collected if variations in hormones is to be determined.

Recent advances in the techniques help in getting accurate estimation of the various hormones. Some of the most sophisticated techniques which have helped in understanding the role of the various chemicals in the tissues and the body fluids are spectrophotometric, fluorometric, chromatographic and radio enzymatic methods. These methods are briefly described here.

Chromatography : the primary goal of chromatography is to separate/resolve a complex mixture of substances into its individual components. As a part of the technique, the sample is introduced into a flowing column of liquid or gas that passes through a bed of particles. The compound that has greater affinity for the stationary molecule will fall behind and the one with lower affinity will get separated. Later on, the various standard methods are used to identify the compounds. The technique allows separation of compounds for a more reliable analysis later on.

Radio Enzyme Assays : These are a form of immunochemical assays where a specific antibody is used as a reagent to detect the unknown chemical or antigen. The antibody or antigen is labelled with enzymes and thus is allowed to react with the antigen to be measured. A substrate of enzyme is then added. The amount of product formed from the substrate by action of the enzyme present indirectly indicates the antigen concentration as it is labelled with enzyme. This is an extremely sensitive and specific technique though slightly expensive. Radio enzyme assay is most commonly used to quantitate concentrations of hormones and metabolites and serve a useful purpose in stress measurements.

Spectrophotometry : In this method the compound to be quantitated is made to react with certain specific chemical reagents under strictly controlled conditions so that the end result is a coloured solution. The intensity of this colour is directly or indirectly proportional to the concentration of the unknown substance. This colour is read off in a spectrophotometer which measures the radiant energy emitted, transmitted, absorbed or reflected by the sample. Because of the low cost involved the technique is very commonly used in biochemical measurements.

Fluorimetry : The technique makes use of the fact that certain biochemical substances have the property of fluorescence eg. absorb light at one wavelength and emit light at another wavelength. This interaction of radiant energy with molecules is called fluorescence. The property of the fluorescence (that the intensity of the light emitted is in direct proportion to the concentration of the biochemical substance) is utilised to measure the concentration of these substances. The method is expensive and also requires caution to guard against non-specific interference.

Summary

In summary, various methods of measuring stress, when used systematically can help in monitoring it in a given situation.

Use of appropriate methodology can help in assessing the impact of any change brought about in an organisation. The change would be in the management practice, design of equipment, schedule of work etc. In clinical practice efficacy of any stress reduction intervention can be established through proper measurement only. For example years of rigorous testing with the help of physiological measurement could establish the efficacy of yogic practice and biofeedback in stress reduction programmes.

Similarly the careful assessment of stress caused by environmental stressors has led to legislations which make it mandatory for people to reduce the stressors to a safe limit. Useful legislatures regulating environmental stress i.e. in work place and residential area have forced people to do a rethinking about design and planning.

CHAPTER 8

HARNESSING STRESS

The main theme of this book has been that a stress-free life is a misnomer and that a proper understanding of the stress phenomenon should help in harnessing it in such a way that it does not cause any undue damage to an individual's functioning in various spheres of life. In order to achieve this goal efforts are required both at macro level as well as at micro level. At macro level certain societal efforts are required to take care of the needs and interests of people for their protection against avoidable stress. At micro level efforts are required to help a person to have a compatible relationship with his environment so that various stressful demands do not cause any harmful effect. Harnessing of stress, however, is in the ultimate the responsibility of the individuals who have to strive to re-structure their lives in such a way that they experience an optimum sense of well-being despite various potentially stressful demands.

The strategies which have been found to be most effective in harnessing stress are broadly categorised under three heads: viz.(a) protective, (b) preventive, and (c) therapeutic. These categorisations have been done more for logical organisation of matter than to communicate a rigid compartmentalisation of strategies. Protective strategies are concerned with steps that are taken to see that people are not exposed to undue stress. Preventive strategies are concerned with those measures which prevent stressful situations from becoming overwhelming. Therapeutic stress management, on the other hand, is concerned with steps to be taken for keeping the stress response within safe limits. In this chapter attempt is made to discuss in detail the protective and the preventive stress management strategies, and the therapeutic stress management will form the content of the next Chapter.

Protective Stress Management

The guiding principle in stress management is that the extent to which people are protected against stress depends on the extent to which the sources of stress are reduced or eliminated and the opportunities are provided for building up of the resources.

The principle suggests a process that would require a constant monitoring of the various sources of stress, keep them under check and at the same time create circumstances which will facilitate a harmonious relationship between the person and his environment. Mental hygiene scientists and the stress experts suggest the following steps to protect people against stress:

1. *Protect people against undue deprivation of needs* : Since frustration of needs is a major source of stress, satisfaction of basic needs is the first requirement for protection against stress. Without the satisfaction of needs of food, shelter, safety from dangers, a person cannot survive. At the same time the satisfaction of a person's psychological needs are also important. People need to establish supportive emotional relations, to experience some challenge as well as autonomy. They also need opportunities for the expression of their potentialities. The extent to which a society will be stress free will relate to the extent to which these needs are taken care of.

2. *Provide opportunities for the development of resources* : Since experience of stress is inversely related to the resources of a person, society should provide opportunities for the development of resources viz. health, knowledge and skills. Here, the basic approach adopted by community health programmes can be well accepted because the effort and expenditure on preventive efforts is the most economical way of ensuring the well-being of people.

Various health programmes can be integrated in schools and the place of work. Experience shows that such programmes wherever introduced, have been successful. To develop the resources of knowledge and skills, opportunities for formal and non-formal education should be provided. Mass media as well as the experience of the members of the community can be utilised for the purpose. The senior citizens in any community can be utilised to develop the resources for the younger generation.

In urban living special care needs to be taken for people to get opportunity to develop intimate relationship by becoming members of a social net work. Highly individualised nature of work and apartment type dwelling units act as deterrent to such relationship building. Provision of playgrounds, recreation parks and attractive open spaces where people can spend time and mix with other people are effective investments towards prevention of stress.

3. *Increase public awareness about high risk behaviour* : Many a time people expose themselves to avoidable stressors because of their own behaviour. Such behaviour has been given the name 'high risk' behaviour. Rash driving is the most common cause of accidents. Similarly consuming various addictive drugs and alcohol bring multitude of problems for the person as well as for others.

4. *Enact laws for the attainment of above objectives* : In any nation both physical and psychological stressors which cause far reaching damages should be eliminated. Where they cannot be eliminated the vulnerable groups should be protected. Laws of the country may not change the conditions but they can act as guiding principles. When combined with deterrent punishments and efforts at making people aware about them to enable them to take timely action, they help gradually by providing enough protection against stress.

5. *Develop systems to provide help in stress management* : There are many problems which are beyond the capacity of an individual but certain social systems can help in protecting people against them. For example, police can protect against assault on life and property. Courts of law act as mediators in resolving many social conflicts. To protect people from homelessness shelter homes are essential. Similarly counselling centres and mental health agencies play an important role in keeping people mentally healthy.

6. *Encourage maintenance of traditions and rituals which foster social cohesiveness and act as natural manifestation of coping with stress* : In modern times there is a lot of criticism about excessive expenditure and wastage of various kinds on rituals associated with various transactions in life. Though there is some justification in these criticisms but there are many rituals which have a very positive value as is evident from the fact that these rituals have survived through centuries. These rituals provide institutionalised ways of coping with unpleasant emotions like anxiety, fear and grief. Most cultures have rituals associated with high stress situations such as birth, marriage, death and other important events. House building, starting on a long journey are marked by special rituals to ensure safety. Collective prayers, feasts and formalised mourning and burial or cremation rites serve the same purpose of coping with negative emotions. These rituals need to be supported and even facilitated by the society so that people are allowed natural expression of their stress.

Preventive Approach to Harness Stress

Preventive approach to stress reduction involves efforts at development of resistance against stress so that stressful situations do not cause any damage. The fact that majority of people are able to survive through ups and downs of life suggests that most people do develop resistance against stress. Yet efforts are needed to ensure development of such resistance, and making people stress resistant. It is possible to prepare people to experience minimum of stress in highly stressful situations through some of the measures being discussed hereunder.

Stress Prevention through facilitating Normal Development

During the entire course of life, development of an individual takes place through discernible stages which occur in a predictable sequence. Each of these stages has its own demands but how well they are met with or how threatening they are, depends upon the development that has taken place during the earlier stage. For example, the traditional Indian thinking divides life into four stages and for each stage the demands are well structured. How well a person is able to meet these demands depends upon his insight, his learning of his roles and the development experienced during the earlier stages. An individual who had a successful and happy childhood is likely to be a stressfree adult.

Erik Erikson, an Amrican psychologist who spent his life studying the course of development during the various stages of life has argued that the successful completion of each stage of development depends upon the match between the social demands and the capacities of an individual. He has coined the term 'developmental tasks' to describe the development which should be completed during a particular stage.

Erikson's Scheme of Developmental Tasks

Infancy : Developing a trusting relationship with mother and learn to trust himself – outcome – hope.

Early childhood : Developing a sense of autonomy controlling own body, communications and control over the environment – outcome – willpower.

Preschool age : Developing an awareness of own role in relation to others, realizing own limitations, accepting them as natural and have initiative to plunge into play activity – outcome – purposefulness.

School age : Mastering the cognitive, behaviour and social skills for adult role as provider and caretaker – outcome – competence.

Adolescence : Developing own identity, based on a review of earlier conceptions, of validating and modifying them to fit into a stable self and the world relationship – outcome – fidelity.

Young adult : Developing lasting relationship of trust and a balance among work, procreation and recreation – outcome – love.

Adulthood : Guiding the next generation and being productive in ways which will sustain the social world – outcome – generativity, caring and widening of concerns.

Old age : Accepting the fact of having lived one's own life. Looking back without remorse – outcome – wisdom.

During formative years completion of development tasks depends upon the contribution of parents and other significant people who help an individual in his development through (a) their warm and caring presence or being available, (b) giving structure to his behaviour by formulating clearcut rules and by providing feedback about his behaviour, (c) helping him to realise that lapses and failures are a part of the developmental process. During adult years the development depends by and large on one's own efforts at self improvement and self steering.

Stress prevention through Anticipatory Preparation

When a person is prepared for a situation he can tolerate it better. This preparation has to be achieved in two ways, (i) through positive social circumstances and (ii) through providing information.

(i) Building of positive social circumstances: We cannot prevent occurrence of stressful situations but we can certainly provide an individual with social circumstances that can counteract the experience of stress. The most important of these circumstances is the emotional support that one can get out of a close-knit social network. Studies on combat fatigue or PSD show that stress tolerance of a soldier depends upon the confidence and trust placed in colleagues and in the leadership. The same condition applies in other situations. Availability of people who can be depended upon in any form of relationship viz. parents, teachers, counsellors or friends can immensely increase a person's stress tolerance. Grand parents do an excellent job in this area. In job situations too availability of opportunity to build close interpersonal relationships reduces the stress of employees. At higher rung of the job hierarchy when executives are provided with professional counsellors they function more efficiently as providers of support to their juniors.

The other stress reducing social circumstances are concerned with social integration. For effective psychological functioning people need to experience a sense of having a rightful place in a social group. Such a sense increases their self-worth and as a consequence they maintain a high morale.

There are several ways in which people get integrated into a society viz. being employed or getting married. If people have a meaningful role to play and they know about it then there is a sure insurance against stress.

It is always wise to make anticipatory preparation and getting ready to face situations known for high stressfulness first because the act of anticipation in itself takes away unpredictability of the situations and secondly because there are simple yet scientifically tested techniques available to prevent high stress. These techniques are commonly grouped under the term stress inoculation because they help in developing resistance against stress. The stress inoculation procedure may vary from a simple ten minute orientation to a prolonged well-structured training programme which can be easily adapted for use by anyone. The procedures involved in these inoculation programmes are described hereunder.

(ii) *Providing Information*: The unknown is always threatening. Getting information about what to expect reduces threat. Knowing about various situations allows a person to cognitively/mentally rehearse the different coping strategies one can employ and get ready to face the actual situation when it comes. It is for this reason that orientation programmes for new entrants whether in education, job, on transfer or hospitalisation serve a useful purpose. For patients going in for surgery information about the type of sensation one should expect has been found to be very useful in their recovery. Patients who know about the sensory experiences do not get panicked about unusual sensation or pain and therefore require less medication. However, since everyone may not welcome receiving information it is advisable to use caution in giving information. On this account people can be divided into two types: the vigilant type and the avoidant type. The vigilant type people are information hungry but the avoidant type prefer to remain ignorant, and hence may be more harmed than helped through information. In any case for providing informations one must use discretion and caution in deciding 'what information' is safe, because everyone may not be able to accept the final diagnosis in a terminal disease.

Use of Vicarious Learning and Modeling to Provide Information: When Armstrong put his first foot on the Moon his blood pressure rose and his pulse rate increased because he was entering into the unknown but later astronaughts had learnt from Armstrong's experience that stepping on the Moon is not a threatening experience. Observing others handling a situation in a calm and confident manner infuses confidence. This principle is used in the modelling technique of stress prevention which involves watching another person enter a stressful situation with no harmful effects. This technique is used most effectively in preparing children for hospitalisation or surgery. Both actual models as well as filmed versions have been used for this purpose. Some of the films prepared for this purpose are:

Linda encounters in the Hospital, UCLA, Instructional Media Library, Los Angeles, California

Scott Goes to the Hospital, Alfred Higgins Productions, Inc. Los Angeles, California

Christine has an Operation, (audio-filmstrip), Wilkins and Saunders, Philadelphia, Penn.

As an example of the use of the live model we may cite the case of the child who is afraid of dental examination being made to watch another child sitting in the dentist's chair and being examined by the dentist. The experience enabled the child to get himself examined without much apprehension.

Increase Tolerance through Stress Inoculation Training (SIT)

The techniques of anticipatory preparation discussed above have been integrated into a systematic training programme by Meichenbaum and Turk to prepare people for high stress situations. The SIT programme is based on the simple scientific truth that when people develop a sense of self efficacy through some sort of preparation, they can regulate their behaviour better. SIT trains people to cope with situations likely to be highly stressful including impending dangers and losses. SIT comprises of a three phase programme: (a) education, (b) skill training, and (c) practice. But before starting the actual SIT one has to plan to identify the specific stressors involved in a situation, the type of impact they are likely to have and if the situation for which one is to be trained is a complex one and has different aspects then a separate training programme has to be given for each aspect. For all complex situations it will be essential to (a) identify the aspects of the situation, (b) the skills required for each aspect, (c) to integrate these skills into the training programme. The three phases of the SIT programme are:

1. *Education Phase* : The objective of this phase is to take ambiguity out of the situation. The learner is given as much information about the nature of the stressors as he is likely to encounter and the impact they are likely to have.
2. *The Skill Training Phase* : Once the learner has been made fully aware about the situation he has to be given training in the use of cognitive skills, so that he develops skills of using self instruction through statements like, 'breathe slowly', 'relax', 'go slow', 'take one step at a time'.
3. *The Practice or Application Phase* : At this phase a simulated situation is created for the learner to apply the various skills he has learned and practised.

Self-help in Stress Prevention

Severity of stress to a large extent depends on the intra-individual factors like appraisal and availability of various resources as well as one's general approach to life's problems. A change in these factors can help in preventing much of the stress. In fact it all starts with a philosophical approach to life that problems and failures are a part of life, they come and go. But the tough people come out of them wiser and stronger. And, if you ask them how they survived them they will provide certain bits of information which can be considered universal wisdom. Whenever there is a problem it is better to see the positive side of the situation. In the worst of situations one can find a new opportunity or a new meaning. In such situations try to compare your circumstances with those who are in circumstances worse than you and this will help you to count your blessings.

Know your own Level of Stress Tolerance

We all have a wonderful capacity to fight the adversities. But this capacity is limited and differs from people to people. So the best thing is to know your own level of stress tolerance and try to keep your stress level within the safe limits, neither too low nor too high. Ask yourself, "How much stress can I tolerate". This question is very important because over enthusiasm to keep the stress level too low may bring the pressure of demands also so low that it can add to stress rather than reduce it. There are several ways of keeping the stress level within safe limits, some of which are as follows:

(a) *Prioritize your goals* : Remember, it is your life, so take stock of your life, your goals and your priorities. Spend sometime on analysing them. Remember also that no one can achieve all that he wants, you too will find that many things that you wanted to do or achieve can be easily given up without significant loss on goals. A simple exercise like the one described below can help you in this task. Take a piece of paper, write down all that you have been striving for and then categorise them as those that are 'very important', 'can wait', and as those 'you can do without them'. Concentrate only on those items that are rated as 'very important', and take only one of these important items at a time. This will gradually help you to find that this way things get more organised and also more under your control.

(b) *Bring predictability in your life* : When an action demands deliberation and conscious decision-making it requires extra effort and this adds to the stress. A regulated routine life on the other hand runs smoothly leaving one free to attend to more important things in life. Therefore, regulate your life in a broad framework of routine so that there is some predictability about it. In the process gradually your system will get so programmed that most of your actions will not demand deliberation and hence extra efforts. However do not make your life so rigid and fixed that even the smallest change can upset you. Avoid major changes in your life and life style while tackling a highly stressful situation. For example, if you are given an additional responsibility in your job avoid making a major purchase like buying a car, changing your residence etc. specially by obtaining loans. These may not be so essential and can wait a while till you feel well settled in your job. In addition if you try to obtain as much information as possible about the new situation you have to encounter, it helps in dealing with the situation more confidently because you know what to expect when the actual encounter takes place.

(c) *Maintain some control over your life* : Every individual has a need to experience a sense of autonomy. Experience tells that even in the most regimented life conditions there is scope for some control over one's life. Cohen, a psychologist who worked with prisoners of war during the World War II and also after the War reports that those who survived the torture of the Concentration Camp were the ones who could in some way maintain a sense of control. These prisoners used a variety of ways of controlling their lives. In one instance, Cohen reports, prisoners just wished the guards forcing them to respond and in this way got a sense of autonomy. The Wakhlu couple who were kidnapped by the militants in Kashmir and were kept as captives for 45 days also report about having used different strategies for gaining control. For example, they maintained their routine of meditation, persisted in their efforts to educate the militants about the Indian point of view and also took upon themselves the parental role for the young militants who were given the charge of looking after them.

They made the most important decisions about their lives themselves instead of completely surrendering themselves to the circumstances and in the process came out successful in their attempt to gain freedom from the militants.

(d) *Enhance your resources* : Since stress occurs when situations cannot be coped within one's resources, the sanest way to prevent stress is to develop and add to the resources. Health, knowledge, skills, finances, social support, alternate modes of coping are some of the examples of these resources which can be developed to help prevent the stress.

(e) *Develop a Healthy Life Style*: Health is among the most important resources of a person which help him to steer through a stressful situation often without much damage. Health makes life enjoyable besides providing strength to cope with life's problems. Common sense says that it is less costly to be healthy than to be ill. Research evidence in recent years has confirmed what the wise always believed in, that the secret of health and longivity lies in a set of specific behaviours labelled as behavioural immunogens because they provide immunity against various health related problems. A person who has developed such behaviours should follow certain health practices/behavioural immunogens:

1. Exercise regularly
2. Have a regular sleep for 7–8 hours
3. Eat breakfast everyday
4. Abstain from smoking
5. Stick to a reasonably balanced diet
6. Maintain weight at or near the prescribed weight
7. Avoid use of alcohol
8. Follow safety practices eg. traffic rules, safeguarding against health hazards
9. Make recreation a part of life
10. Read health related materials (this increases awareness and motivation for maintaining health)

These simple rules are not difficult to follow. Once adopted, they become a part of life style.

(f) *Develop skills and knowledge*: In the modern times of knowledge explosion there is a constant pressure to update one's knowledge and skills. It does not mean that you load yourself with unnecessary knowledge but useful knowledge comes handy in all critical situations. The most important and useful knowledge is about the various resources that are available and the manner in which they can be tapped. If you know "where to go for which problem", you will be making life much easier for yourself. Update your professional knowledge and skills through some extra reading or join some short term courses in the area of your specialisation. But professional or not, certain skills will always come handy. Make a list of skills you need to develop (do not try to be a Jack of all trades). You can always find people who can help in developing these skills. An individual's survival today depends on skills in the use of technology related to his field of operations. Learn these skills as fast as you can. Whenever you purchase or obtain any gadget, read carefully about it and about its mode of operations and functioning – may this gadget be an electric toaster or an advanced level computer. If you don't learn about them you shall have to depend upon others and accordingly lose control over the situation.

In social situations the most common yet preventable source of stress is not having proper communication skills. People often get so much baulked down by emotions that they fail to communicate what they actually want to communicate. The most dangerous situation is that of pseudo communication which occurs when the parties concerned think that communication has taken place, when in reality it has not. If you have to face specific situations repeatedly where you experience difficulty in communicating your ideas, you need to prepare your script, rehearse it and then use it in an unemotional way. Gradually it will become a habit with you and you will be communicating what you mean to communicate. Also learn to saying 'no' to unreasonable demands of others, parents, children, colleagues or the boss. Practise seeing things from the other person's point of view. The world does not look the same to everyone and this can be learned through practice. For example, in some medical colleges doctors are encouraged to get admitted as 'in-patients' incognito and experience what a patient goes through during illness in the hospital. These doctors report much better functioning in interpersonal situations after their experience as they are able to empathise with their patients. Use of positive emotions — hope, faith and humour has an immense capacity to counter stress. There is, therefore, need to rely more on these emotions.

(g) *Enlist support from your family and friends* : Big problems cannot be faced alone, so seek support from your friends and family. They can help both in keeping your morale high as well as in making an objective assessment of the situations.

Hans Selye thinks that most important stress prevention strategy is to try to 'earn thy neighbours' love'.

(h) *Count you blessings* : Life is a mixture of happy things and not so happy things (hassles). If you reflect on unhappy things you will be unhappy, but if you reflect on the happy things you will be genuinely happier. In one study psychologists divided a group of subjects into two groups. These two groups of subjects were given the same questionnaire.

One group of subjects was asked to mark the happy events (daily uplifts) and the other group was asked to mark the sad things (hassles). After some time the two groups were asked to rate their level of distress. You may have guessed correctly. The second group rated itself more distressed than the first. You can draw your own conclusions from the study.

When you feel highly depressed compare yourself with people in less advantageous position than yourself. You will surely find yourself consoled.

(i) *Lastly Develop a Sense of Humour* : All positive emotions relieve distress, and humour is the most positive among these. Try to stretch your lips in a smiling position and you will feel lighter. So when you genuinely laugh your spirit will definitely rise. Here the experience of Normal Cousins is worth mentioning. Cousins developed an incurable disease and was advised hospitalisation. Instead he preferred to be in a hotel watching humorous movies. Gradually he started improving. He did two things — maintained a close contact with his doctor and tried to be cheerful. With these two things he could fight his ailment. Gaining insight from his own experience he could help thousands of people to fight illness. You too can practise to look at the lighter side of things and prevent much stress in life.

Summing up

The simple rules discussed above are time tested. Anyone who adopts them is bound to have stress within tolerable limits.

CHAPTER 9

THERAPEUTIC STRESS MANAGEMENT

Whenever people go through any traumatic experience or are living a life full of hassles that affect them overwhelmingly, they need some help in the management of the situation in such a way that exposure to it does not cause any undue harm. And, if it has already affected them, they must be able to counteract the effect. The most commonly observed harmful effects, as we have seen, are in the form of cognitive insufficiency, worry, anxiety, irritability or body symptoms like muscle tension, aches and pains etc.

The therapeutic help provided under these circumstances aims at removing the stress, its cause or reducing the discomfort caused by it. While in Chapter 8 we have discussed the protective and the preventive methods to deal with stress, in this chapter we shall be dealing with methods that are therapeutic in nature. This implies that therapeutic methods are to be applied when the individual is already experiencing stress. The stress causing situation has either already occurred or is right here. A variety of methods have been devised for this purpose. However, there is no method that can be called the 'cure all method.' This is simply because of the complex nature of stress itself. In any given situation, the success of a method would depend upon the nature of the problem causing stress, the nature of the individual going through stress and the skills of the person giving the therapy. Here it may be emphasised that often an otherwise efficient method may fail because the therapist has not considered all dimensions of the problem. On the other hand a very complex approach may delay the process so much that it is not effective. Some times a therapeutic effort may also fail because both the psychological and physical aspects are not taken into account.

The best approach therefore would be the one that allows for the exigencies of the situation and the capacities of the therapist to choose the method of therapy. Take for example the case of a man who is transferred to a new department at a time when his marriage is on the verge of breakdown. He starts complaining of headache, sleeplessness and exhaustion. Here symptomatic treatment is not the complete solution. What the man requires is the help first in sorting out the issues related to marital disruption, secondly he requires the permission to continue in the old job till his family life is stabilised.

The therapeutic stress management programme comprises of scientifically tested ways of helping a person to overcome or reduce stress to a tolerable limit. Any programme with the intention of reducing stress has to be carried out by agencies or individuals who are specially equipped to provide such a help. The therapeutic approach may sometimes take into account the entire situation or it may be limited to either increasing tolerance for stress or to eliminating physical and psychological symptoms of stress. A brief overview of the methods commonly adopted for this purpose is given here.

Counselling – A Holistic Approach

Counselling is the most commonly adopted method for helping a person in distress. But counselling is possible only when the person under stress is ready to discuss his problems with the counsellor and reflect over them. In fact the concept of counselling implies that the individual being counselled has a capacity to sort out his problems with some supportive help.

Informal counselling has been used by people throughout the ages and has been found quite effective. Such counselling is available to people from friends, parents, teachers etc. But professional counselling can be provided only by a person

Fig. Walking and jogging are simple forms of exercise.

trained for the purpose. A professional counsellor has the advantage of being an outsider who can look at the other person's problems objectively and provide help without getting emotionally involved in the situation. A professional counsellor finds it easier to build trust since the client knows that the counsellor has no personal interest at stake. Throughout the process he acts as a powerful source of support.

How does a counsellor help? In most situations a counsellor adopts a problem solving approach. He helps the client analyse the situation and identify the source of stress. Then the counsellor and the client together work out a strategy and a plan of action. Once the decision has been made, the counsellor supports and even facilitates action. The approach is holistic since it takes a total view of the circumstances.

Often counselling has to be supplemented by other stress management techniques for either increasing stress tolerance or for reducing stress response.

Techniques for Increasing Stress Tolerance

There are innumerable situations in life that are a constant source of stress, yet they cannot be changed by an individual. Under these circumstances the wisest thing is to adopt an approach that will help him to tolerate these situations and thereby decrease the chances of letting stress have an upper hand. Stress tolerance techniques help in increasing the physical capacity or in developing resistance against stress. These techniques are discussed under physical fitness programmes.

Physical Fitness Programes: Physical fitness programmes are based on the fact that good health and physical fitness can increase a person's general endurance. Of course going through such programmes cannot remove the source of stress but it can, to a large extent counteract the effect of stress by generating a sense of well-being. People engaged in sports or otherwise going through some sort of physical fitness programme often admit that after going through these activities they feel elated, relaxed and calm. Moreover, physical exercise leads to a decreased heart rate, improves utilisation of blood sugar and reduces fat. Most importantly exercise helps in reducing blood pressure that is a common ingredient of stress response.

In modern high technology settings where increased leisure itself is a source of stress, exercise seems to be the most viable solution for the stress problem. Otherwise also, a regular exercise programme distracts attention from the various problems. Many people who do regular exercise as a part of some fitness programme observe that they have become aware of their body parts for the first time. As they go through these programmes regularly with increasing agility and flexibility their self concept is also enhanced. One feels 'good' even by looking at one's healthy body. Physiological researches show that during exercise brain releases certain mood-elevating chemicals that create a sense of well-being. This should be the sufficient reason to include exercise in a stress management programme.

A positive self concept and a sense of well-being along with increased tolerance prevent a breakdown under stress. In support of such a programme we may refer to the statement of an exercise enthusiast, Dr. Fred Stutman, who has popularised walking as an exercise. Recalling the experience of a day when he walked the deserted streets after a long and gruelling work at the hospital, he states, "I suddenly realised that I no longer felt tense or tired. All the worries about my patients' illnesses, as well as, my own personal cares seemed to evaporate as quickly as the smoky vapours of my breath in the frosty night - my spirits were raised and my blood pressure went down."

The experience of Dr. Stutman is no exception as the statements of any regular exerciser will tell. However, the exercise plan must be chosen according to physical health, interests and convenience of the individual. A simple guideline is given here for the convenience of the reader.

1. If a person is not used to physical activity and has been leading a sedentary life medical consultation is essential. A simple medical check-up will help in determining the extent of strain his system can bear.
2. Always start at a very low level of exercise and then gradually increase it to the optimal level. For example, if a person decides to follow a schedule of running or jogging but is not used to them, he should start with a schedule of short regular walking and only when the body

is conditioned to take up vigorous activity should he start jogging or running.

3. Regularity is more important than vigour. A small amount of daily exercise is better than a vigorous but erratic programme. The daily schedule should also include a day of rest. For example it could be 15-20 minute exercise for six days with one day's rest.
4. Most importantly, exercise should be done in a pleasant frame of mind, then only it will stimulate the stress counteracting processes in the brain. Never carry out an exercise programme in a competitive spirit. Often without realising, people may compete with themselves when they are not competing with others. Remember, all types of competition add to stress instead of reducing it. This is because competition releases adrenaline, an important stress hormone. A brief introduction to 'easy to carry' aerobic exercise follows.

Aerobic Exercises: The most commonly recommended exercises are aerobic exercises. These exercises involve vigorous contraction and relaxation of various muscle groups. The advantages of these exercises come from their rhythmic nature. The most popular forms of aerobic exercises are walking, jogging, swimming, skipping and cycling. When these exercises are carried out at a certain rate over a long enough time there is a rise in body temperature, increase in heart rate and breathing rate with a greater supply of oxygen to body cells.

In the 1970's and the 1980's aerobic exercises or aerobics were developed into rhythmic gymnastics and their popularity almost became a fad. Their utility gradually came under a shadow of doubt as their vigorous workout plans were sometimes found quite damaging. However there is no doubt about the time tested simple aerobic exercises like walking if they follow the basic principle of moderation, regularity and pleasant outlook.

For anyone not used to walking, a fifteen minute schedule on alternate days for six weeks is recommended. After this it can be raised to 30 minutes, gradually it can be increased to 45 minutes to one hour. The speed can be 3km to

A simple plan for walking

1. Like all exercises, in walking also medical check-ups ensure safety for beginners.
2. Walking should be avoided immediately after the meals.
3. While walking one should wear properly fitting clothes and footwear.
4. Walking should continue only till one can walk without strain.
5. Walking should be smooth with energy being put in every step. After sometime a natural rhythm will emerge.

5km per hour as the individual feels comfortable. Whenever one feels tired one must rest for a while. Walking must never be done in a spirit of competition.

In modern times urban people hesitate to go out for walking or jogging. Good exercise cycles are available in the market for such people. Guidelines for following a schedule of cycling are also supplied with them.

Techniques Aimed at Lowering the Stress Response

The second strategy to overcome the effect of stress strives for lowering the stress response itself. Because of lowered stress response the individual is able to go through the stressful situation without adverse effects both at mental as well as at physical level.

Two routes are followed in these techniques. One can either start at a physical level and lower the psychological response as well or one can attempt to regulate the psychological stress response and in its course also lower the physical response. The techniques adopted in pursuing these two routes are discussed separately followed by a more global approach.

Techniques with Emphasis on Lowering Physical Stress Response

As everyone knows from experience the most common manifestation of stress response is in the form of tension in the body musculature. The tension may be experienced in the form of either generalised condition of the body and appear as general lethargy or as localised tensions. When prolonged it results in unpleasant sensations that are perceived by an individual as aches and pains such as low back pain or tension-headache etc. Therapeutic management of these problems tries to reduce this very tension through various relaxation techniques. The therapist tries to train a person to relax various muscle groups of the body. The task is not always easy because often the habit of "tension" has been there for such a long time that it becomes an integral part of one's behaviour. Under these circumstances a person trying to relax may become more tense.

However it must be remembered that no one can remain relaxed for ever. On the contrary some degree of tension is essential to help a person function efficiently. Hence, all that these relaxation techniques can do is to prevent tension from becoming excessive. Since these techniques promote general physical fitness they provide a sense of well-being that becomes a part of a person's general feeling. Some of these time tested techniques that are considered relatively safe are:

Massage

Massage is perhaps the oldest method used all over the world, for removing muscle tension. One reason for the popularity of beauty parlours and health clubs could be that they include some period of massaging in their programmes.

Massage is not only a physical therapy, it is a mode of communication that uses skin, the largest sense organ with touch as a means of communication. (The value of touch lies in the intent with which it is done. A touch with the intention to give tender loving care makes the other person feel cared and loved.) Through appropriate strokes it helps a person to become aware of one's body, listen to what it has to say and thereby understand what it needs. For example during the massage one may realise that certain parts of the body are completely frozen or some muscles are totally atrophied. Consequently, one can focus on improving the functioning of these parts.

The pleasant sensations experienced during massaging tend to have a euphoric effect and therefore generate a sense of well-being. The secret of generating such a feeling lies in the loving and caring touch. Because of this reason the attitude and intention with which massage is given are very important.

At physiological level massage hastens the blood circulation, tones up muscles and helps in releasing of toxins.

Through experience one can judge as to which strokes are comforting for a particular individual. In this way it can be adapted to needs of that individual. Some therapists have tried effectively, giving an under water massage also. The client is made to lie in a bath tub filled with gently warm water and then massage is given. The added advantage of an under water massage comes from the fact that all sensations except those coming from the massaging are cut off.

Caution: Like all other exercises massage should be avoided immediately after a heavy meal. It should also not be given on an area that is injured, inflamed or is painful. At most a gentle touch may be applied to the inflamed area. If massaging causes pain, one should be encouraged to go in for a medical consultation.

Relaxation Therapies

Relaxation therapies are based on the logic that stress or tension and relaxation cannot exist together in the system. Several research studies show that when individuals undergo relaxation therapy their (a) immune system functions more efficiently and they are equipped better to resist various diseases (b) the heart and vital organs function better and (c) a sense of well-being is experienced. A variety of techniques are available in practice. While some of these concentrate on muscle relaxation, others focus on breathing or even use an integrated system. For any type of relaxation therapy a quiet place and comfortable position is the primary requirement.

(a) *Progressive Muscular Relaxation:* This technique was devised by Dr. Jacobson in early 1930's and has been popular since then. It is called progressive muscular relaxation because the technique requires relaxation of muscles one by one beginning from the toes and moving towards the head.

An abbreviated format of the instructions for the progressive muscular relaxation is given below.

The instructions given here are an abbreviated version of Dr. Bernstein. Minor modifications may be made after developing an expertise in the method.

Instructions: Begin with the right (or the dominant) hand.

Arm: make a tight fist, Keeping the upper arm relaxed. Let go.

Upper Arm: press elbow downwards against the chair. Let go.

Repeat for the other hand.

Forehead: raise eyebrows as high as possible. Let go.

Neck: counterpoise muscles by trying to raise and lower chin. Let go.

Chest, shoulders and upper back: Take a deep breath, hold it and pull shoulder blades together. Let go.

Abdomen: Counterpoise muscles by trying to push stomach out and pull it simultaneously. Let go.

Dominant upper leg: Counterpoise large muscles on top of the leg against the two lower ones (Variations are allowed). Let go.

Dominant calf: point toes towards head. Let go.

Dominant foot: point toes downwards, turn foot in and curl toes gently. Let go. Repeat this for the other leg, calf and foot.

(b) *Relaxation Techniques Based on Yoga:* Yoga and its various versions are the most popular techniques of stress management. "Yoga" is considered a way of life that aims at attaining self realisation through meditation, the highest form of mental activity. Yogic exercises were originally meant to prepare the body for such sublime existence. The stress management experts have realised the potential value of yoga for attaining relaxation. The Vivekanand Yoga Kendra has devised a short programme for this purpose. It attempts to stimulate and then bring about physical and mental relaxation. The programme comprises three forms of shavasanas, four standing asanas and three sitting asanas.

Since the various asanas should be learned under the guidance of a teacher to avoid any harmful effects only the shavasanas are being described here. Shavasana by itself has an immense relaxation value and can be practised safely. The shavasanas have to be done in a lying position.

Shavasana Type-I

Lie supine, join the heels and the toes. Join arms at the sides of the body. Tighten the heels – tighten the ankle joints, stretch the calf muscles...

Pull the knee caps – tighten the thigh muscles.
Exhale and pull the abdominal muscles inwards.
Form the fists – tighten them – stretch the arms.
Inhale and expand the face.
Tighten – Tighten – Tighten.
Release and relax.
Legs go apart, arms apart, palms facing the sky.
Allow the whole body to relax and collapse.
These instructions should take 30-45 seconds.
Total time to be spent 2-3 minutes.

Shavasana Type-II

This form of shavasana has three phases. Before beginning, the person should lie down on the ground with the back totally, resting. Let the whole body collapse. Instruct to keep the legs apart, arms away from the waste, palms to be facing the sky.

This asana involves getting a 'feel' of the body.

Phase-I *Observe Abdominal Muscles:* Feel the abdominal muscles bulging up and sinking down, Count 10 cycles.

Phase-II *Associate Muscle Movement with Breath:* Try to notice that inhalation is associated with upward movement of abdominal muscles and exhalation with sinking down of the same muscles.

Feel the deep breath down the lungs and feel exhalation as emptying the lungs. Do not force breathing; observe the natural breathing.

Phase-III *Associating Breathing with Feelings:* Try to experience that every time you exhale, the body gets relaxed and every time you inhale, the body gets energised. Repeat observation for 10 cycles. Normal time taken should be 3-4 minutes.

Shavasana Type-III

Part by part relaxation: the deep relaxation technique.

Instructions – Lie supine on the ground with hands and feet apart, palms facing the sky.

Focus attention on all the parts of the body one by one.

Focus your attention on toes, ankles, calfs... on the head.

Feel that each part is relaxed.

Focus your attention on the toes – feel that they are relaxed.

Feel that your toes are relaxed. Now feel your feet relax.

Continue suggestions for each part of the body till head.

After sometimes the individual will be able to use self instruction to attain relaxation.

Guidelines for the Instructor

The instructor will do well to get a training from a yoga expert and give guidance to the clients. Let them carry out the relaxation under supervision till they have gained complete mastery of the technique.

The yoga practice can be done either in the morning or in the evening. The clothing should be light and lose. It should be done on empty stomach or after only a very light meal.

(c) *Autogenic training:* Utilising imagery and auto suggestion for getting relaxation.

Dr. Jonathan Schulz, a pioneer in behaviour modification firmly believes that our bodies function as self regulatory systems and that if anything goes wrong, the brain can trigger the corrective activities. A remarkable thing observed by Dr. Schulz was that these mechanisms can be given a command to carry on these corrective activities. His techniques called autogenic training makes use of this phenomenon only. It makes use of auto suggestion to counteract the influence of stress.

When clients come to a clinic for the treatment of stress related symptoms, they are encouraged to give auto suggestions so that they experience conditions that are opposite to stress symptoms, i.e. heaviness and warmth of extremities, regulated cardiac functions and breathing, warming of abdomen and cooling of the forehead. The technique makes use of auto suggestion rather than any active effort. Step by step instructions are as follows.

> Begin with making the client lie in comfortable position. Make suggestions about heaviness, i.e. "your left leg feels heavy, your right leg feels heavy, your left arm feels heavy", and so on. . .
> Next, concentrate on breathing. Say, "your breathing is getting relaxed."
> Make the client repeat the instructions for himself, i.e. "my legs. . . . etc.
> Now give suggestions about mental relaxation, i.e. "your mind is getting relaxed, your tensions are getting removed. You are feeling extremely calm." Ask the client to repeat these statements. Once the client becomes adept at all these statements he/she can use these whenever there is a need for temporary respite from stress.

The autogenic suggestion can be embedded into a pleasant image. For example the client can be encouraged to imagine a pleasant scene like a beach, a garden or the bank of a river. Integrate into the imagery everything pleasant, e.g. the temperature, the breeze, the smells and the sounds. With a little practice it becomes a part of one's habit and can be used anywhere anytime.

d) *Biofeedback – An Extension of Autogenic Training:* The biofeedback technique is applied when the stress is manifested in the form of specific symptoms like headache, asthma or hypertension. It is the most sophisticated use of the scientific knowledge of psychology and an individual's ability to attain self control through auto suggestion. Alleviation of specific symptoms may not be possible merely by the use of more generalised therapies like aerobics and they have to be supplemented by more rigorous therapies like biofeedback targeted at removing these symptoms.

The technique of biofeedback makes use of psychological processes, e.g. auto-suggestion to regulate physiological processes although it is not easy to regulate the involuntary processes. Like autogenic training, biofeedback also can be classed as a technique of behaviour modification. It makes use of a kind of learning known as operant conditioning. This type of learning takes place when a spontaneous response gets reinforced in some way. For example a child encounters a particular aunt and spontaneously smiles, the aunt then cuddles the child (which makes him feel good). There is a probability that next time when the child meets this aunt he smiles on her. In other words, response that is spontaneous otherwise gets conditioned and tends to be repeated because it has been reinforced. Here the individual gets a 'feed back' that it is a good response. When this principle is used as a sophisticated therapy, the client is provided a feedback about his physiological processes and a `good' physiological response gradually tends to be repeated with increasing frequency. In the course of various researches and in various stress management clinics information about temperature, muscle tension, blood pressure and perspiration rate have been used effectively for providing the feedback. Because of these biological indicators being used as feedback, the therapy is known as "biofeedback" therapy.

Therapy through biofeedback specifically aims at three things,

Helping the client to (i) develop an increased awareness about internal processes; (ii) be able to gain a control over these processes; and (iii) ensure that the awareness and control developed in the laboratory is carried over to the real life situations. The treatment in the laboratory usually makes use of sophisticated instruments for giving accurate information about the changes in the physiological processes going on inside the body. Gradually the clients learn to monitor and become aware of the various internal states associated with changing physiological process. This helps him to recognise as to when these processes are within the normal range and therefore feel good about them.

For example, in a simple experiment nurses provided their hypertensive patients with their blood pressure readings repeatedly over a period of time. Gradually the diastolic and systolic blood pressure readings for these patients came down. These patients could recognise their normal blood pressure that motivated them to keep it within this range.

As a matter of fact any physiological indicator for stress response that is giving trouble can be used as a feedback. But most frequently used forms of feedback are GSR (Galvanic Skin Resistance) which gives "information about electrical conductivity of the skin". This is because the conductivity of skin increases when wet and decreases when it is dry. During biofeedback training electrodes are put on the fingers and change in conductivity is communicated through sound signals. Other forms of feedback used are visual display about muscle tension level, blood pressure level or heartbeat.

The most successful use of biofeedback training has been in the treatment of tension headaches that is a common manifestation of stress. When someone is having a tension headache, there is a rush of blood towards the temples. As a result of which, hands get cold. A patient is trained to raise the hand temperature and thereby feel a relief from headache. Reginald Beech a psychiatrist from Manchester, England reports on effective use of such a treatment with his patients. He reports that many of his patients could later function effectively without getting tension headaches. The highly motivated persons can benefit by getting a relief from high blood pressure also.

A common use of biofeedback is for treatment of anxiety symptoms. Professor Sargunraj reports that he has been using electromyograph for an effective treatment of anxiety. The strength of biofeedback lies in the fact that the instruments used are highly sophisticated and therefore can provide information about the minute changes in physiological functioning. Usually it does not have any adverse side effect. However if a symptom serves as a means of coping with a stressful situation, a symptomatic treatment will not serve any purpose. For example, if a child who often feels neglected and is able to get parental attention on complaining of a headache or an employee who can escape from an unpleasant job situation because of the headache are not fit candidates for biofeedback training. In such cases other options may be judiciously chosen.

(e) *Meditation for Relaxation:* Meditation is an ancient technique that was originally used for the purpose of attaining intuitive insight into the higher reality. Many versions of this technique are available and are prescribed by various religions throughout the world. The use of meditation for relaxation is of recent origin and has been used effectively both in the laboratory as well as in the stress management programmes.

Meditation more than all other relaxation techniques, requires a comfortable position and a quiet atmosphere. It also requires a passive approach where a person does not fight with the thought or emotions. A regular breathing and uncritical attitudes on their own quieten the thoughts and emotions.

How to meditate

Sit comfortably, regulate your breathing and focus your attention on the breathing itself. If you wish you can say some words of prayer and go on repeating the same words as long as you wish.

The other alternative is that you listen to a sound repeatedly so that your breathing gets tuned to the regular sound.

Dr. Andrew Goliszek suggests the use of metronome sound for this purpose. Another alternative is what Zen teaches. You concentrate on the thought process itself. Let the thoughts flow without attempting to stop them.

Inclusion of meditation in a stress management programme is highly recommended because it trains us to use our inner resources to tune ourselves to be relaxed. When carried out for a limited period regularly it is pleasurable and safe. With regular meditation we get into the habit of being relaxed and therefore are able to go through high stress without having an adverse effect. The next section deals with techniques that reduce psychological stress response.

Techniques with Emphasis on Lowering the Psychological Upheaval

As stated in the beginning of the book the psychological upheaval is the most disturbing aspect of a stress response in the form of intrusive unpleasant thoughts and emotions. Because they interfere with rational thinking they must be controlled when aroused to a stressful level. Two types of techniques are used for this purpose e.g.. use of chemicals and cognitive therapies. Both of these have their advantages and limitations and therefore have to be used with discretion.

(a) *Use of Chemical Therapy for Controlling Stress:* The overwhelmingly widespread use of drugs to alleviate unpleasant reactions associated with stress suggests that they are sought as a quick and easy solution to one's problems. These drugs are used to regulate both the emotions and the cognitive processes. According to various estimates they are the most maligned, misused as well as the most prescribed drugs.

When stress is acute and symptoms like severe depression, suicidal tendencies and/or extreme withdrawal are present, use of prescription drugs may become essential. But self medication with these drugs is dangerous. Some of these drugs in their natural form have been a part of our culture for a long time. Even then their use is never recommended.

Drugs have their own disadvantages also. Because these drugs stimulate certain brain centres, they are habit forming. The result is that people tend to use them even when they are not prescribed by a physician. Some times people can develop true physiological dependence. In such cases discomforting physiological symptoms appear, forcing them to continue using these drugs. When taken for a long time people develop tolerance for them and have to take increasingly larger doses. All drugs have some side effects and cause harm when taken beyond safer doses.

The most valid reason against the use of drugs is that their use interferes with the process of `habituation'. Take the example of a situation when a major grief strikes a family like death of a significant person. In situations like this people go through a process called `grief work', i.e. crying, talking or reliving the important events related with the person. A photo album may be taken out, one may go through the belongings of that person. These activities help in coming to terms with the loss. Under such circumstances if certain drugs are prescribed to provide relief from the sorrow, the suffering may continue for a much longer time. Drugs may be prescribed by a physician only when there is a risk of further damage due to trauma caused by a stressful situation.

(b) *Cognitive Approach to Stress Management:* Cognitive approaches to stress management involve active efforts to bring about a change in the cognitive processes. Behind these efforts, there are at least two important reasons. First, as you have seen, when people are afflicted with stress, their cognitions become the first victim. You will recall that because of the narrowing of attention during stress, many important cues coming from a situation are missed. As a result our cognitions about a situation are distorted and the judgements about them become faulty. Coping efforts based on misjudgments naturally become ineffective. These faulty cognitions have to be changed if an individual has to be helped to cope effectively with the stressful situations in his life.

In simple terms these techniques involve bringing a change in the pattern of `self talk' to reduce stress. It is a common experience that unless we are busy with some complex mental activity a flow of thought goes on as if an audio tape is being played and we find that we are talking to ourselves. This has been given the name of Self Talk. This is a normal activity of the brain, but whenever some negative emotions are aroused, this self talk becomes self defeating. Statements like "I will kill you" or "I am doomed" only interfere with the thinking and therefore reduce efficiency of an individual. Cognitive therapies try to change this phenomenon to allow the individual to function efficiently. Among the various techniques used for this purpose two are worth mentioning. These are `cognitive re-structuring' and `thought stopping'. Because of their simple nature, these two techniques are being described in brief.

(i) *Cognitive re-structuring:* As the name indicates the technique of cognitive re-structuring attempts to bring about a change in the thoughts in such a way that they do not cause emotional upset. As an example take the case of a parachutist who gets frozen at the moment he is about to jump. This is because the moment he is about to jump he tells himself "what if my parachute does not open?" The thought is enough to freeze him. If it happens once it is OK, but if it happens every time he attempts to jump he needs to change. He may be helped through cognitive re-structuring. An analysis may show that not opening of the parachute is a rare phenomenon and that he has been trained to meet such eventualities if at all it happens. Very often negative self talk becomes persistent and continuously interferes with efficient functioning. A person can be helped to analyse the situation and assess it by asking oneself "is there a basis for such a thought". And then look for positive facts and deliberately incorporate them in the self talk. For example a student with fears of failure can be helped by learning to tell himself, "I have studied hard, I am well prepared for the examination, so I am going to be successful".

(ii) *Thought stopping:* The other technique called `thought stopping' uses a more aggressive approach. The client has to be trained to use self instruction to prevent unpleasant thoughts from coming into the focus of attention. It is a three-step technique. (1) Disturbing self statements are identified, (2) the client is made to repeat the statements, (3) after a few repetitions, as the statement begins the therapist calls out "stop" and the client stops at that point. The exercise is repeated several times. At the next stage the client also has to call "stop" which has to be a self instruction.

Thus, a stupefying stress causing self talk can be reduced. But the client may also be helped to understand that all self talk can neither be stopped nor does it need to be stopped. It is only after a thorough analysis of one's thought processes that one has to identify which self talk should be stopped or replaced with a positive self talk.

Multimodal Therapy

At the end we may agree with Richard Lazarus that since stress is a complex problem it needs to be approached in a 'multi-faceted' way. He has termed this approach 'multimodal therapy'. Lazarus suggests that when a person is having a severe stress its various aspects need to be handled by methods in which all aspects of the problem are taken into account. Take the case of Deepak who tended to remain tense and gradually developed hypertension. At the back of his problem was his lack of assertiveness due to which he was facing problems in his job. He was feeling weak and exhausted. He needed a therapy that took care of the cause of the problem and its various manifestations. The therapy would involve counselling, behaviour modification, relaxation, assertiveness training and drug therapy for his hypertension. In addition, a regimen of exercises and proper nutrition can be of immense help to Deepak.

Summing Up

The therapeutic techniques discussed here are simple and may be applied by anyone with a little understanding and interest in the well-being of others.

CHAPTER 10

SOCIAL SUPPORT – AN IMPORTANT MEDIATOR OF STRESS

We have started with the basic premise that the experience of stress and its consequences depend upon one's ability to tolerate and manage stress. Several factors contribute to this ability. These factors function through interaction with the person's environment specially the social environment which has been built through ages to safeguard against the various stressors a person encounters in his life. The significance of social environment becomes evident from the fact that man and his ancestors have lived in close-knit informal social groups. These close-knit social groups comprise of individuals who are simultaneously members of several groups which serve different functions in their life. (see box)

> On getting up in the morning Rajeev spends some time with the family. At 8:30 A.M. he goes to school and spends time with his classmates and the teachers. At lunch time he enjoys eating with a group of his close friends. Rajeev is also a member of the District Football Team. Sometimes he works as a member of an environmental protection group. On holidays he goes to attend the religious congregation of the faith, his family follows. Rajeev is simultaneously functioning as a member of several social groups.

Through such multiple memberships groups are form a network of social relationships and as a consequence every individual becomes a member of a social network which become a part of his personal life. His behaviour is regulated by the demands put by the groups in the network, the role he plays in them and the succour he seeks from them. Once a person becomes a member of a network he strives to maintain it even at some cost. This desire to build and maintain a social network serves a special function in the survival of a person.

When humans arrive in this harsh unpredictable world, they need close personal contact to go through the harshness of a strange world. It is through the care and nurture provided by the first and the primary social group (the family) he belongs to, that his survival is made possible. Gradually he is able to fend for himself but the need for others and the desire 'to belong' becomes so ingrained in him that he is willing to pay for maintaining the relations that form a part of his network of inter-relationships.

Social Inter-relationships and Social Support

Social support is a special condition of inter-relationships which makes one feel worthy of someone's concern and also generates the feeling that the other persons too feel for him the same way. For example, when one gets support from a teacher, a doctor, a counsellor or a parent the situation provides for a sense of worth to both, the one who receives support and also those who provide support. (A large crowd in the ante-chamber and various expressions of gratitude are certainly ego-boosting for any professional.) The feeling of self-worth generated in this way gives an individual confidence that he can rely on the inter-relationships he has built in the course of his life.

The supportive relationships a person can rely upon at any particular time emerges out of the social network of which he is a member. Since a person's social network comprises of all the attachments he has, it includes all of his social resources and his support system emerges out of this network of social resources which may comprise of several of his friends and relatives and also some professionals. It may however be noted that at the time of stress he seeks support only from a few chosen ones and not from all those who constitute the network of his social resources. (see Fig. 1)

The figure shows that a person chooses at a point of time only a sub-system from the network of his support system and within a particular sub-system also some persons may be very close like family members while with others relationship may be relatively superficial. In the former case relationship is marked by reciprocity and emotionality of a high degree. But in the case of not so close relationship also, the person may feel that he is being supported. However, in case of others like with the professional people relations have minimal reciprocity, e.g. we do not expect our doctor or lawyer to confide their problems in us. This point gets clearer with an understanding of what social support is or constitutes.

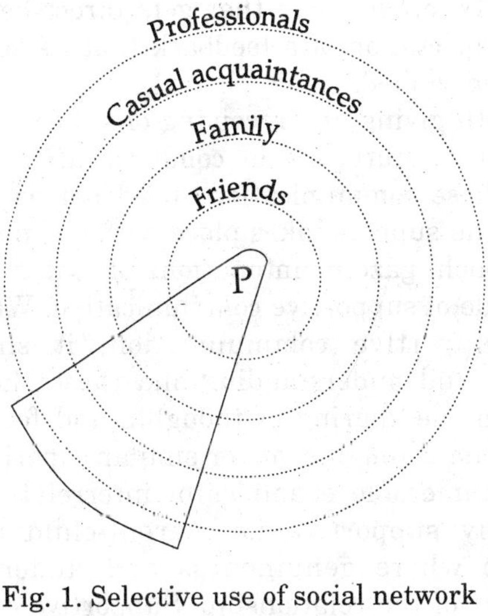

Fig. 1. Selective use of social network

What is Social Support

Social support is a special condition of mutual relationship. When people come to know in some way that there is someone who is willing to be of some use, they feel supported. Since this condition emerges out of social relationships it has come to be known as social support. Cobb, a pioneer in the study of social support describes it as a set of information which makes him believe that (a) he is cared for and loved, (b) he is valued and respected, (c) he is part of a network of mutual obligation and communication. It works like this: from the behaviour of the other person one gets the information that there is someone who loves and cares for him, and in return for the love and respect given, the other person puts him under certain obligation i.e. one comes to think, "If I can take his time and energy he also expects the same from me". When the other person uses this right he adds to one's sense of self worth, that is, 'I am important to him'. In this way we can say that social support is a special condition of inter-relationship which is based on mutuality of commitment and communication. When people form any relationship they expect some benefit out of it, more so in supportive relationship wherein some benefit must come to both the parties. In formalised supportive services where one party works for the sake of providing support to the other party that gets direct benefit, there is atleast an expectation of a feedback that its services are appreciated and valued.

Since both giving and receiving of support depends upon communication, mutuality of communication becomes very essential. These communications need not be always verbal as much of the support takes place without the use of words. Gestures, touch, gaze or intonations of statements are more common mode of supportive communication. Whatever be the mode of supportive communication, it should involve genuineness and understanding and these should be made evident from the sharing of thoughts and feelings of those who have gone through same or similar experiences. We can think of innumerable examples of interrelationships which are mutually supportive i.e. parent-child or friendship relationship where genuineness and understanding are inherent part of the relationship. Supportive communication involves:

a. genuine information seeking/giving
b. spontaneous problem solving
c. empathytT— sensitivity towards other persons' thoughts & feelings and,

d. equality — mutually expressed positive regard & tolerance.

What Social Support does to Us

From our personal experience we can know whether an intimate relationship is supportive or not. A supportive relationship seems to fulfill the basic survival need. Soon after the child is born the contact with the mother and prompt satisfaction of its needs lays the foundation of such a relationship. Every time an infant looks up it meets the gaze of its mother and hears her voice giving re-assurance that it is safe. Possibly such feelings of security are carried over to all relationships which communicate warmth and concern. Gradually such experience of warmth and concern become essential for the psychological survival of a person. When others show concern and are willing to do something for us we feel valuable in that our existence has a meaning for others.

Before we take up the issue of what social support does to reduce stress we should look at its value for our general well being. We can say for sure that social support builds a positive environment and is growth producing. We feel good when we know that we are wanted and valued. It needs no experiment to prove that a happy family and congenial atmosphere at job make us feel good and enhance our sense of well-being. (Don't you feel good to know that your family cares for you?) There seems to be an inbuilt mechanism which brings about positive feelings when there are supportive people around us. Endocrinologists suggest that pleasant stimuli in the environment stimulate a positive brain system activity. Reinforcing stimuli like affection, sex, social approval, touch, eye contact and other social support indicators seem to act on this system. Most probably they release chemicals known as neuropeptides. The response triggered by this system is opposite to the Cannon's flight-fight response and brings about an euphoric effect, that is, an individual feels generally elated and relaxed.

Availability of social support is growth producing at any stage of life. As an example we may quote the studies on premature neonates. These neonates are considered to be high risk babies and are usually kept in hospital nurseries. If mothers are allowed to handle and feed them, there is marked improvement in their growth (in terms of weight gain and a decrease in mortality).

Not only physical growth but growth in other areas is also facilitated through social support. For example, in an early study in a research organisation Pelz showed that scientists who worked under supportive supervisors showed maximum growth. The style of functioning of these supportive supervisors comprised of daily contact with the juniors and yet allowing them independence in work. These findings can be easily validated through innumerable evidences of what a supportive teacher and a supportive manager can do for the personal growth of any person. Such a role becomes evident from the studies on unemployed youth. In the course of a project unemployed youth were encouraged to form a club so that they could pool their resources of contacts, skills and information. Through mutual help and concerted efforts the members of the club were able to get employment.

In another research project, youth who had an erratic job history i.e. always leaving a job and getting unemployed were helped to retain their job successfully through continued support from friends and supervisors. In terms of psychological growth children brought up in a supportive home are generally happy and take interest in play, study and work. Such advantage of support as stated above is always there, stress or no stress. The strength gained through such experiences stands a person in good stead in stressful situations also.

Social Support as a Mediator of Stress

There is mounting evidence to show that social support is the most important resource a person has for managing stress. For example, during major disasters if children are rescued along with their parents they come back to normal without evidence of any damage. Among adults also when people can share their experiences they adapt fast to the losses suffered. Only the lonely and those without having any available support have problems. In other situations also people having strong social support do not show much of after effects of stress. For instance, in job situations people who are doing highly stressful jobs, if allowed to develop friendship relationship do not suffer from after effects. Similarly during plant shut down unemployed youth who belong to a network of relations and friends are able to tide over stress better than those who lack such support.

The most important evidence about the value of social support in stress reduction comes from the researches in health field. These researches repeatedly show that, after experiencing major events, availability of social support helps prevent adverse health loss. For example, after an adverse life event like bereavement or loss of job, people who are surrounded with friends and relatives regain their well-being faster than those who have to struggle alone.

Absence or loss of support is often predictive of development of serious illness like coronary heart disease (CHD), cancer or depression. These facts have been repeatedly verified. Observations on migrant groups suggest that once they lose support from people, illness takes hold of them. For example, Japanese in their native place have a low risk for CHD. They also live in close-knit communities with strong network of interrelations. The same people, when they migrate to America tend to have a high incidence of CHD in spite of the fact that there is no change in diet pattern and life style. All that had changed was that they had lost the support from their close knit families. Like the migrant population, men and women admitted to old people's homes who are deprived of the close bonds with friends and relatives show adverse effects of stress. For these people both the mortality and the morbidity rates are much higher than the same age people living in the community. The sad case of old people admitted to old people's home shows that the best of physical care and comforts in an impersonal home cannot replace or compensate for the loss of support of friends and family.

Psychological study of cancer patients and of persons with mental health problems present a similar picture. Studies on cancer patients, similarly demonstrate that among the susceptible people, that is, those who develop cancer, are generally lacking in supportive relationship during their early life. The case of people with mental health problems is not very different. Such people have been brought up usually in homes lacking emotional warmth and supportive relationships. In their current functioning also it is seen that as the size of the network increases for these people, the number of problems they face decreases. The inverse is also true, that is, if the network becomes smaller problems they face increases. But in the case of women who develop depression the findings are a little different. A series of research studies emphasise the value of quality and not merely the quantity of support. These studies show that when women experience serious life events, the only protection against depression is a single close relationship with husband or a boy friend. Women who have a large network of not so close relations, on the other hand, are not protected, if all other conditions conducive to depression are present. Social support not only helps in prevention of stress related illness, it also helps in recovery from an illness. The case of Norman Cousins is worth mentioning here.

Norman Cousins an editor of a well known news magazine developed a life threatening disease. Instead of submitting helplessly to the disease he put a remarkable fight against the disease. His struggle and then success has become a well known case of an unusual partnership between a patient and his doctors. In his auto-biography 'Anatomy Of An Illness' Cousins says, "I was fortunate to have as physician a man who was able to put himself in a patient's position". Through his support Dr. Mitzig helped Cousins to use his own powers of 'laughter', 'courage' and 'will to live' in almost total recovery from his illness so much so that instead of being invalid, he could rejoin his job and function efficiently.

Two Ways in which Social Support Works

There is no doubt that social support is the most important mediator of stress. Whether or not a stressful situation will have an adverse effect depends upon the availability of a number of factors and among these factors social support is the most important one. Now the question is, how does social support operate that stress does not have any adverse consequences. From our study of scientific literature and also a look around us we find that social support operates through two channels to reduce stress, (a) through creating a positive environment (direct effect) and (b) through being a stress buffer.

The direct effect of stress is best seen when people feel secure and good because they are wanted, loved and liked by others. When we know that there are people we can rely upon, it generates a sense of well being in us. Although such direct effect is not always evident due to several factors operating in our lives at any point of time, yet whatever evidence that is available shows that as the number of friends and relations increases, there is an increase in one's well-being.

The positive emotions experienced through contact with others provide an "affect balance" which helps us to go through stressful situation without much damage being caused. Just as when we have a bank balance, great financial difficulties do not upset us simply because we have something to fall back upon. The biochemical evidence also suggests that when social support is available stress response occurs at a reduced level. Biochemical analyses of blood during stress response shows that there is a rise in the hormones known as corticosteroids. These hormones show a rise among monkeys when they are taken out of their cage (Being out of cage is a stressful situation.) But there is no such rise in hormones when mother and infant monkeys are together taken out of the cage. Similar evidence is obtained in fear situations also. Human and monkey infants do not demonstrate fear response when they are clinging to their mothers. Possibly this is so because direct effect operates at the stage of primary appraisal since the effect is such that the situation is not stress producing.

The other pathway through which social support operates involves the modifying of the stressful situation in such a way that stress is not allowed to have any adverse after effect. This function of social support is known as stress buffering function. Since social support operates between the occurrence of a stressor and its after effects, the buffering role may be seen as an aid in coping which acts throughout the stress process by (i) reducing the demand and lowering the threat, (ii) getting ready through anticipating the threat, (iii) providing a more objective assessment of a situation so that coping occurs, (iv) providing aid in actual coping or (v) helping in reducing the stress response through distraction. A few examples of each of these stress reducing function will be helpful.

Reducing demand: A supportive person can reduce the demands on a person going through a period of high stress, and thus help in bringing down the stress within the tolerance limit. Depending upon the exigencies of the situation different steps can be taken to reduce stress. Parents looking after the basic needs of their children or becoming lenient about their participation in domestic chores when they are working hard for some important examination or wife taking up a job when husband is facing financial difficulties are examples of some of the steps taken to reduce demand.

Anticipatory preparation : A supportive person decreases severity of stress by providing predictability to the situation. Because an advance warning can help a person to make anticipatory preparation, a teacher announces a class test well in advance, a manager explains about the overtime schedule a week ahead of actual implementation, a doctor explains to the relatives the serious turn a patient's illness may take.

Provide an objective view : Since high stress may bring about distortions in perception which interferes with correct assessments of the situation, a supportive person may help in making a more objective assessment of the situation so that the source of stress is correctly identified and tackled. For example, a counsellor helps a client to overcome the denial, a doctor helps a patient to overcome the panic and adjust to an illness in a realistic way.

Help in coping : Support can come in the form of actual coping, when the supportive person takes over the responsibilities of the person under stress temporarily. Examples of such coping are when the nursing staff take over the responsibility of daily routines in cases of seriously ill persons or children take over the responsibilities at home. As the person recovers and is in a position to resume his responsibilities, support is gradually withdrawn. At this stage encouragement, persuasion and even coercion may be helpfully used.

Keeping the arousal level low : Finally, the supportive person can help create a situation in which a very severe stress is not experienced. Various tension reduction techniques are used for this purpose. Cheering, joking, distracting or being available and building faith are some of the ways of providing support. This function is most effectively carried out by all the psychological therapies which make use of supportive relationship as their technology. Mystics, Shamans and the tantriks too, in the same way act as a support. In treating their patients both the psychotherapists and the traditional faith healers carry out this function. The faith invoked in the tormented person reduces anxiety and invokes positive emotions. The calm and confident way of facing a problem is also contagious and is unconsciously adopted by the person under stress. Sharing of thoughts and experiences is helpful though it is an elementary supportive situation.

In summary, social support helps to reduce stress as well as to prevent its adverse effects. Presence of social support safeguards one's physical and mental health. However, there are situations when social support rather than reducing stress may add to one's stress. The increase in stress may be in several ways, i.e. by adding to the cost of support, by adding to the stress or through a mismatch between the need and the support. All supportive relationships involve mutuality and whatever the donor does in order to help a person, puts the recipient under some obligation. If the cost of meeting the obligation is more than what a person can afford, it may add to one's stress. If a friend who has helped you in some emergency, desires to use your car every other day, it adds to your fuel bill and your resentment against the friend.

Because support involves closeness of relationships it may be regarded as an intrusion upon one's privacy since by sharing of thoughts one has to open up about one's anxieties, worries and other negative thoughts. At the same time knowing about the other persons' affairs, problems and achievements adds to one's own burden e.g. when a good friend's family is going through hard times it becomes difficult to ignore it and the friend's problems add to one's own burden. Problem may come from over enthusiastic support also. If the supporting person is over imposing it can deprive a person of the sense of control which is very essential for a person's survival. Sense of control comes from successful mastery of a difficult situation through active coping. When a person makes active efforts to cope with a problem he takes an overview of the situation, takes into consideration several strategies and chooses one. But when other person makes this choice for him, he loses the sense of mastery or the feelings that he is the master of the situation. Such a situation of over support brings about dependence. In extreme cases it develops a sense of helplessness in a person.

Rational choice and support seeking: The support system comprises of all the resources a person has access to, and this is built through active effort of the individual over the years. The process of support building starts almost from the beginning of life. Very early in life infants have to send through their gestures, actions or words, a message which will invoke a positive response in other individuals. Cooing, smiling and maintaining an eye contact with the mother as well as with other care givers are the rudiments of support seeking behaviours. These behaviours gradually develop into special modes of coping with stressful situations. Turning to others, sharing of thoughts and feelings are examples of coping modes adopted when no other solution to a problem is in sight.

However people do not seek support indiscriminately. Before seeking support from anyone people make a cost benefit analysis of the support. Only when the benefit from the support is likely to be greater or equal to the cost that support will be sought or given. For example, a student facing difficulty in his course work would not seek support from his teacher if he is made to unnecessarily wait for several hours or has to suffer some other kind of humiliation which hurts more than the benefit he can receive. Similarly, if the teacher feels that giving help to the student will add to his burden more than the satisfaction he will get, he will avoid helping the student. Besides the cost consideration, discretion is used in choosing the support since different types of support serve different purposes (see Table 1).

Table 1. Types and functions of support

Type	Function
Ego support/ Emotional support	: Enhances self worth, raises morale
Cognitive support	: Clarifies doubts, facilitates anticipation, helps in objective evaluation of a situation
Material support	: Provides objects or materials required for coping e.g. money, books, medicine, transport etc.
Instrumental support	: Provides actual help in coping with a stressful situation

Ego support/emotional support is required when people are feeling demoralised and disheartened. Cognitive support is needed when stress so overwhelms a person that the perception about the situation gets distorted. Material support, on the other hand is required when a person lacks the means to cope with the problem. But very often what is required is actual help in solving a problem, in fighting a case, writing an application, going to a doctor etc. Here an instrumental support is required.

The following example should explain how support involves active effort and rational choice making. Mr. and Mrs. Varma are new arrivals in a neighbourhood of middle class people. Once they are settled in their new home they spend time meeting people and establishing neighbourly relationship and gradually they are able to establish a small network of friends. Once when Mr. Varma met with an accident and was hospitalised, his neighbourhood friends rallied round the Varma family. As the period of hospitalisation got prolonged Mrs. Varma approached the treating doctor to get a correct assessment of Mr. Varma's condition and on knowing that Mr. Varma will need a long treatment she contacted Mr. Varma's employer to seek financial assistance. She also contacted her old employer and requested for a job so that she could carry the financial burden. Mrs. Varma also requested one of her relatives to come and stay with her and help her in carrying out the added burden of Mr. Varma's illness. Mrs. Varma could reach out to these people as the Varma's had built up a network of social support.

The above example shows several things, (1) support systems do not emerge spontaneously: they have to be built with efforts over the years, (2) once support systems have been built they remain there and become operational during times of stress, (3) out of the network of relationships discretion has to be used in choosing the source and the type of support that is needed, i.e. who can provide which type of support.

Who Can Provide Support

Every individual living in a society has at least some capacity to provide support. Support giving is built in our nature very early in life. As helpless children we begin to identify with care givers and in the process learn to provide support to others. All it needs is some degree of empathy or ability to see things from the other persons' point of view. Empathy is a perceptual ability which comes with experience while interacting with other people. When we interact with others we realise that meaningful interaction is possible only if we are able to see things from the other person's point of view, in other words, without being a participant in the experiences we should be able to live through the other person's joys, and sorrows, worries and successes. Possibilities of empathy increase if we are aware of the other person's circumstances. Hardship of a miner is different from that of an airplane pilot or a farmer. We can appreciate their hardships only if we know their circumstances or atleast have a motivation to understand them.

The other important ability required is to get the other person convinced of the genuineness of one's intents. For example, if the other person feels that we are policing despite the fact that our intention in approaching him is to provide support, we will not constitute his support system and hence not considered supportive. Both research and clinical observations show that if we can reveal a little of our own self, the other person will be able to have confidence in us. Perhaps some self disclosure on the part of the donor makes the receiver of support feel that the donor is also a human being with emotions and weaknesses, therefore it is okay to rely on him. People who avoid self disclosure are seen as secretive and untrustworthy. Such people are not good at providing support.

Besides being trustworthy, appearing trustworthy is also important. Similarity in experiences make people more acceptable as supportive. For example, during adolescence peer group is considered to be more fit to provide support than persons belonging to older generation. Many professional persons are specially trained to provide support to people in need. In all societies there are many formal and informal agencies working for the goal of providing various forms of support to people. These agencies need to be strengthened as well as utilised for helping people under stress. Various well defined systems which have been recognised as sources of support are: (a) organised community groups such as religious groups, schools, clubs, trade unions and various voluntary organisations, (b) self-help groups like alcoholic anonymous and PTA, (c) formalised supportive services like foster homes and old age homes. Other agencies in a society which provide support are police, judiciary and healthcare systems although their help is sought only as a last resort.

Who are the People who Lack Support

In spite of such a variety of support available in a community there are people who lack support. Since support seeking behaviour is a major factor in getting support, a person's skills, needs and network are important in determining whether or not a person gets support. Persons who have a need for affiliation and a feeling of helplessness try to build social networks and get supported in times of need. On the other hand a very high feeling of self-reliance is detrimental to network building. For example, people living in modern urban setting who are overloaded with demands of living get apprehensive that if they maintain relationships their load will increase. City people are in this way motivated to move towards self-sufficiency. Such people neither initiate nor have informal support available to them. When people lack some of the social skills, such as communication skills, empathy or self-disclosure they get isolated and live a lonely life. People who have a negative self evaluation too can be put in the same category. As these people are apprehensive about revealing some negative aspects of themselves. They think it better to avoid social interaction than to open up with people. Similarly people who are without a family like the unmarried or the widowed get less support than those who are integrated in a family e.g. grand parents in a joint family.

Integration in the society provides opportunities in other ways also for getting support. For example, whereas an employed person gets support from his fellow workers, the unemployed and the retired ones are deprived of this opportunity. Likewise isolated people also lack support. Isolation can come because of social rejection by others, demands of works or because of living arrangements. Many individuals choose to live in isolated areas but others become isolated perforce and not because of their choice e.g. people living in high-rise buildings are often forced to get isolated. The problem becomes more acute when they live in higher floors. Most of these modern buildings are designed in such a way that once people get into their houses, they lose all chances of interaction and therefore they are deprived of building support systems.

Isolation also comes when people get uprooted from their place of origin and migrate to other places either by force of circumstance or to look for greener pastures. The new environment comprises of strange people with stranger ways. If they migrate to an urban area, the demand for adaptation with a variety of new situations forces people to remain aloof till they feel totally comfortable and adjusted. Even with best of efforts it takes four to five years to get integrated into a new culture. If such people migrate in groups they continue to have support otherwise they have to struggle alone.

People also lose support as they grow old. To a large extent it is due to declining physical ability. But shrinking of interests also contributes to their isolation. Unless they are living in joint families where there are grand children, they tend to be isolated. But some elderly people who actively participate in community life — religious, recreational and welfare activities are able to continue functioning as members of a supportive network. Because absence of support has been clearly found to be detrimental to mental and physical health, mental health professionals, while helping the clients in negotiating with many life's problems, help them essentially in building supportive systems.

The Building of Social Support

The important role that social support plays in promotion and maintenance of well being of the individuals makes it imperative that some measures be adopted to ensure that people do have support available. Some of the methods adopted by mental health professionals are worth recording so that anyone interested in helping people can devise his/her own programme. Since people who lack support are deficit either in need for support, in social skills, in social circumstances or the supportive network, programmes can be worked out for development in these areas. Modern learning theory of psychology shows that people can be made to learn every possible thing so why can't they learn to desire and to maintain a supportive network?

People can be made to desire social interaction through pleasurable encounters with others. Since much of our behaviour depends upon the reinforcements we get, a positive tendency towards support seeking can be built through rewarding such behaviours through reinforcements like smiling or patting. It has been observed that when people are put in congenial groups they gradually shed their inhibitions and start interacting. Such interactions can initiate the building up of a supportive relationship.

Social skills such as empathy and communication have been successfully taught through role playing. The procedure involves putting people in simulated situations where they are made to practise certain skills. Five steps which can be modified to suit the needs of the situation are: (a) Instructions and demonstration; (b) Practice through role playing with other partners or role reversal; (c) Feed-back about one's role performance; (d) Repeat role playing; (e) Home practice to encourage transference. If a person experiences high anxiety he can be systematically desensitised to social situations.

When the problem is not related to one's skills and abilities but to social circumstances, because of which informal support is not available, support can be provided through formal supportive services like counselling centres. A counselling centre can provide both emotional and instrumental support. When a person is going through serious crisis half-way homes or residential facilities have to be provided. Short stay homes for women, children and the older people are expected to carry out this function. Such centres can be successful only if they have a warm and caring atmosphere, otherwise they do more harm than good. Research studies show that the warmth of atmosphere emanate from the top. The extent to which the staff is given autonomy in decision making and the extent to which the management shows concern for their needs and welfare, decides the amount of warmth they show towards their wards. Another strategy successfully utilized for support building is the forming of self-help groups of people with similar needs. Self-help groups have been found to function effectively with groups as varied as parents of children with special needs, cancer patients, alcohol and drug addicts, housewives and unemployed youth. When such groups are formed they serve two important functions, (i) allow sharing of thoughts and feelings, (ii) pooling of resources. People from different backgrounds bring different resources which can be used by the members to solve their problems. Resources may be as varied as writing skills, contacts with employment agencies, relatives who can train in job seeking, appearing for interviews etc., and conveyance to take people to employing agencies. As an example we can cite the success story of Haryana village women who decided to fight out the problem of their husbands' alcoholism. These women formed self-help groups to picket the liquor shops and to prevent their menfolk from drinking. These women were successful in getting the liquor shops removed from their village as well as in checking the menfolk from battering and harassing their womenfolk. A lesson for everyone.

CHAPTER 11

INDIAN VIEW OF STRESS AND COPING

The experiences of people — both happy and sad — as well as behavioural response to these experiences are moulded by the cultural template which gives it a unique shape. This applies to the experience of stress and the mode of coping normally adopted by the people belonging to a particular culture. In this context, an attempt is made to present here the Indian view of stress and coping so as to provide a better understanding of stress problems in Indian setting.

The modern psychology conceptualises stress as a dynamic state of the individual which occurs in response to the demands which overtax its capacities and resources. At psychological level these demands are mediated by the appraisal of the situation as a threat to the well being. The threat may come because of the unfulfilled needs, unresolved conflicts, ambiguities, uncertainties or dangers of various sorts i.e. harms, losses etc. In other words stress occurs because of a dynamic interaction between the external and internal forces.

Traditional Indian view of stress is very similar to this yet it is different. The forces operating to create the stress as you will see are conceptualised in a different way. This makes it imperative that one understands the world view which conditions the Indian psyche, the needs, threats, strivings and the perception of the barriers that block the need fulfillment.

The Indian view of life is design oriented. Hence all events in the entire creation are seen as predesigned and as having a pre-set goal. The other important concept is that the entire creation and therefore man also like all other living beings has originated from the *Brahman*, the *Parusha* or the Almighty who is the ultimate reality and who had created life out of playfulness (*lila*) but desires the living beings to go back and re-merge into this reality and thereby attain *moksha* or *mukti*. The concept of *moksha* or *mukti* can be interpreted as salvation or transcendence. *Moksha* or *mukti* is the ultimate goal of life. It is a state which implies freedom from the cycle of birth and death. Experientially it means attainment of a state when an individual experiences oneness with the "ultimate reality" from which he has originated.

In Indian thought the nature of reality is also conceived to be different from the western view. All reality is considered to be a subjective reality which means that all experiences are subjective in origin. The external reality is false therefore non-real. The cognitions about the external reality, infatuation with it or striving for externally determined goals (of attaining knowledge) lead to 'false knowledge'. Therefore, for getting real knowledge an individual has to look within oneself whereby one can get the knowledge about the entire creation for he is a part of the creation — separated for a while yet destined to get submerged with the originator.

In this way the basic theme of Indian thought is polarity between separation and fusion. In explicit words it can be said that with birth comes separation from *Brahman* who is the originator, yet through life after life one strives to go back and get merged into *Brahman* or the supreme reality by attaining *moksha*. The cycle of birth, life and death goes on till one attains *moksha* and thereby get freed from the cycle of life and death. *Moksha* is the condition consequent upon attainment of a state when a person is able to experience oneness with the entire creation. The individual in this state becomes one with the creator. The state is variously described as "thou art this' and "I am the *Brahman*". It is a state of being wherein an individual realises that he is a soul in the body. According to Indian thought life is meant for striving to achieve this state. However, with birth comes various desires which demand fulfillment. As a result the man is neither able to cognise the ultimate purpose (attain *vidya*) nor is he always able to strive for it. The sequence of events is like this: a man (or any other living being) is born, lives a life, suffers throughout and dies; then is born again. The cycle goes on till the man attains the ultimate goal of *moksha*.

Against this background, we can discuss the stress concept. In the ancient Indian literature, there is no term strictly equivalent to the present day concept of stress. Two terms which come very near to it are '*dukha*' and '*klesha*'. '*Dukha*' as traditionally used, is opposite to well-being. It includes all negative feeling states of apprehension and disappointment and hence is equivalent to suffering. So great is an occupation with *dukha* in Indian thought that often the very life is equated with *dukha*. It forms the central theme of Budhism.Budha taught that:

> Birth is suffering, decay is suffering.
> Disease is suffering, death is suffering.
> Association with unpleasant is suffering.
> Not to get what one wants is suffering.
>
> (Humphreys, 1951)

Klesha on the other hand refers to the worldly affairs. Let us explain it in this way — there can possibly be two states in which an individual exists i.e. *Klishta* (being involved in worldly affairs) and *aklishta* (not being involved in wordly affairs). *Klishta* or afflicted state refers to a state emanating from worldly desires and desire prompted actions. The state is marked by all the emotions associated with worldly transactions. It causes misery because it interferes with the ultimate goal of life i.e. attainment of *moksha*. It is because of this reason that *klesha* or the forces which operate when a person is involved in the wordly affair are identified as 'hindering load.' In modern psychological terms we may equate *klesha* with barriers in a blocked goal situations.

Kleshas are a hindering load because of their motivational properties. It means that by prompting an individual to get involved in worldly affairs, they pull a man away from the path of self-realisation or the cognition of oneness with the creator, the Absolute or God and result in *avidya* or non-cognition.

All cognitions about the worldly things which occur through sense organs amount to non-cognition or *avidya*. True knowledge or *vidya* on the other hand comes only with the realisation of an intuitive insight into the ultimate reality.

According to Patanjali 'the moment cognitive processes start emanating from various sense organs the ability to cognise the higher reality is lost and a state of non-cognition sets in'. The loss of cognition that one is part of a great reality leads to an egoistic thinking i.e. "I" and "mine" feelings. And then come attachments leading to severe emotional upsurge. A similar thought is expressed in the Gita:

> 'A non-cognition of pure self gives rise to ego. This veils a man's divine nature from himself. The result is attachment (to worldly things) and compassion which makes a man helpless and impotent.'

Both the above thoughts indicate that stress in the form of *klesha* is a manifestation of a state where non-cognition prompts worldly desires.

Dukha on the others hand occurs because of a constant underpining for the supreme goal. The idea reminds one of the Freudian concept of unconscious operation of a rigid superego which causes a severe guilt when a person is striving for the id or ego related goals.

The striving to go back to one's 'Origin' continues whatever a man does. In this way '*dukha*' or stress is constantly experienced.

The sankhya and the Budhist concepts of stress can be explained through the following flow diagram.

Avidya ⟶ *Klesha* ⟶ *Dukha*
(non-cognition) (desire prompted action) (stress)

The concept of stress as indicated here is process oriented. Dukha here includes both the negative emotional states as well as whatever causes such a state (i.e. *klesha*).

The state of functioning when *dukha* occurs can be equated with the state of non-self-actualisation in Maslow's need hierarchy stystem. According to Maslow human needs are ar-

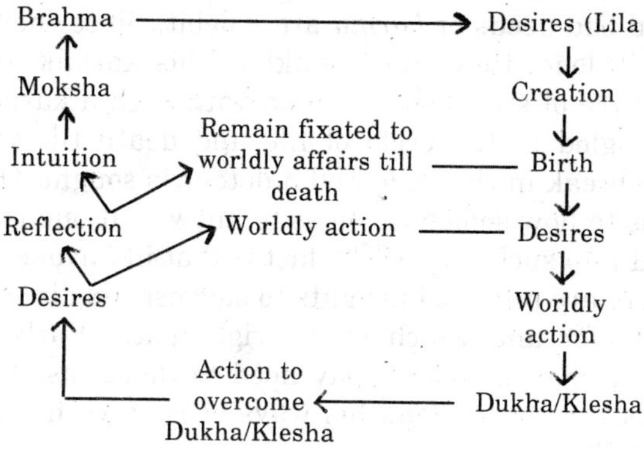

Cycle of birth, life death and moksha

ranged in a hierarchical order with needs from the lowest to the highest. The nature of functioning of a person also differs with the needs which determine the major strivings of a person. A man striving for the satisfaction of his physical needs behaves differently from the one who is striving for the satisfaction of intellectual needs like curiosity. In this context Maslow has suggested that the highest form of functioning is a state wherein a man is able to utilise all his potentialities — it is a state of self-actualisation. But when a man is struggling with lower needs only, this state of self-actualisation cannot be achieved and sense of nonfulfillment may persist. Coming back to Indian thought about stress, it implies that any thought, action or desire which prevents him from the cognition of the penultimate reality of the highest self (oneness of the *atman* and *Brahman*) or from the attainment of oneness with one's source (*Brahman*) leads to stress. A natural corrollary of this idea is that even pleasure and enjoyment of wordly "goodness" is a source of stress.

Another source of stress or its absence explainable through a concept unique to Indian thought is that of '*karma*'. It is a sort of banking system of good and bad deeds, in other words, karma. Good deeds are the deeds carried out without any ulterior motive or desire for some personal gain. These include all deeds carried out with a sense of duty i.e. duty towards others as well as towards oneself. Bad deeds are opposite to them. In this way good deeds or *karma* are a credit and bad deeds or *karma* are a debit. Since they add to the karmik load, they add to dukha. This karmik load is a potent source of stress since a man with such a karmik load gets entangled in the cycle of life and death till somehow there is a break in the cycle and a detour is sought. One may wonder as to how someone comes to know that one is getting entangled into such a web. The fact is that in anyone's course of life there are repeated insights to suggest the direction one is heading for and which is the right path. Early or late whenever a man is able to pay heed to these insights he is able to seek ways to mend his ways or cope with the stress in an effective way.

To sum up stress or *dukha* occurs because of a conflict between the natural pull of the ultimate goal and the force produced by the involvement with worldly affairs (*klesha*) which create an overload. It also occurs because a man has to bear the load of his bad deeds (*dush-karma*) which produce stress either in the form of increased attachment to the worldly things or in the form of sufferings and the miseries.

With this picture of stress in view we can shift attention to the problem of coping with stress. The above analysis should make it clear that the problem of stress is an existential problem since stress according to Indian view is related to the meaning and purpose of life itself and the coping efforts have to be concentrated either on preventing or at overcoming '*dukha*'. This view also implies that life is a closed situation i.e. once born man has to live and suffer at the same time. Yet he has to strive in such a way that he moves towards the ultimate goal of attaining moksha. Because involvement in the worldly affair is a source of stress, this involvement has to be kept to the minimum.

Two potent questions arise in this connection. Firstly, how does an ordinary mortal recognise this exalted goal? Secondly, how can he carry on his life's affairs and keep the level of *dukha* low?

The philosophical treatise suggest that in all human beings there is a natural tendency to strive for this ultimate goal. It is asserted that inspite of its being camouflaged under the cover of non-cognition or *avidya* there is an inner force which keeps reminding him of the ultimate goal. This force operates at a subliminal level while the mundane activities of life occupy the sensory apparatus. The functioning of these forces is unconscious in the sense that a person does not have a volitional choice in their operation. The functioning of these forces can be compared to the operation of id forces posited in the Freudian psychology. Like id forces these forces tend to enter the focus of attention at one time or the other. An individual who becomes aware of these forces gets motivated to work accordingly. This may explain how a person suddenly decides to renounce the worldly pleasures and become an ascetic or a *sanyasi*.

Besides getting an accidental glimpse into the real purpose of life, one can cognise it through a deliberate effort following a three step procedure clearly described in the "*Sankhya*". These steps are reading of scriptures, reflecting over the knowledge attained through reading them and then doing meditation. Since scriptures are written by enlightened persons, reading them spontaneously initiates the process of self-reflection. Frequent sessions of self-reflection followed by meditation do provide opportunities for getting a glimpse of the inner reality which is the true reality. The experience is extremely blissful and therefore reinforces the desire to spend more time and effort to live in that state and strive for the ultimate goal.

Now we come to the second question mentioned earlier i.e. how to achieve the ultimate goal? Before going into the details of the answer to this question let us put a complex situation for reflection. Suppose you ask someone to suggest the best way to achieve success in life and the other person tells you to set your own goal and then strive for it. The suggestion may appear to be pretty vague but this is exactly what the wise men in India ask one to do for achieving the ultimate goal. The fact is that there is no single path to this goal and the Indian philosophy suggests that every one should choose one's own path to the ultimate goal as well as one's own strategies for either coping with *dukha* or to free oneself from the *kleshas*. In a way life is a double bind situation, which means that every event is predestined, yet it is asserted, that man can choose his own destiny in such a way that whatever he does is the result of his own doing. Modern psychology also has developed a concept similar to this i.e. the concept of 'internal control' developed by Rotter. According to this concept people with an 'internal control' belief tend to think that they are incharge of a situation. In fact such people tend to think that they are incharge of their entire life. According to the classical Indian thought it is the duty of every individual to develop an 'internal control' through being a *yogi*. The *yogi* is one who is either in the process of realising or has already realised his oneness with *Brahman* the absolute power behind the entire creation. Patanjali has asserted that yoga is the means of overcoming *dukha* due to *klesha*. He asserts, "Resort to yoga to reduce *klesha*, for achieving higher states of consciousness and for developing higher capabilities" (Patanjali Yog Sutra (11-2).

Yoga is explained as a way of life which disciplines a person for the higher purpose of life. Five types of yoga have been recommended. These five types of yoga are not alternatives to one another but are complementary in nature in the sense that one has to follow the other to give the true benefit. The five forms of yoga are, "*Hath yoga, Karma yoga, Jyan yoga, Dhyan yoga* and the *Bhakti yoga*. Among these *Hath yoga* is most well known to people working in the field of stress management. A brief introduction to these five forms of yoga is given hereunder.

Hath yoga comprises of a series of exercises which provide a readiness for other forms of yoga. The second form of yoga is Karma yoga or the yoga of action. Karma yoga may be equated to behavioural coping or behavioural strategies aimed at minimisation of dukha. Karma yoga is nothing but selfless action as is clearly described in the Gita.

> 'But who-so-ever controlling the senses by mind engages his organs of action in karma yoga without attachment, he excels (Gita 111/7) and... always perform action, which should be done without attachment, for, by performing action without attachment, man attains the supreme'
>
> (Gita 111/19)

Karma yoga does not comprise of mere action, because man will always act. Since he has a natural tendency to act – Karma yoga is doing right action without getting troubled by joy or sadness. It will serve the purpose of keeping the stress level low only when it is in the right direction. In Budhism right action or the action which leads to the right direction holds the central position. Budhism is a religion of action therefore the most important place is given to 'right action'. Right actions help in accumulating the good 'Karmas'. Budhism clearly prescribes what right action is but Hinduism expects a man to find for himself what right action is. It starts with the faith that every man has an inherent capacity to know the 'right' from the 'wrong'. A person with superior intellectual capacity should be able to know what action is right. However it may be difficult for a person with an average intellect to do so. For such an individual the guiding principle is 'dharma' or duty, what ever is one's duty has also been made clear. Two guiding principles have been laid down to decide one's duty which are described below.

Firstly the duties have to be according to the role one is carrying on at a particular time, that is, the stage of life and the role one is playing in a social group. The value of duty is clearly stated in the Gita.

> 'He who carries out his duties without thinking of the fruits of action – he is a sanyasi and a yogi, not the one who has renounced the world".
>
> Gita (VI/1)

The above statement clearly suggests that it is not only the right action but the spirit in which it is undertaken that matters in taking someone towards the ultimate goal.

The sages of ancient India realised that no fixed tasks can be prescribed for people occupying similar positions because societies undergo change with times and even at any particular point of time role expectations may differ from place to place. They clearly stated that one should follow the cultural norms of one's own social group. By following the norms of the social group one is freed of the conflict between the right and wrong. Looking from this perspective the job of a hangman is as righteous as that of a teacher for both are acting according to the requirements of the respective jobs they are holding. What matters is that whatever one does must be done in a selfless spirit. Only then will it lead to life without dukha (or stress) and also add to one's good karmas. An individual engaged in the yoga of action (karma yoga) constantly monitors one's actions in terms of right and wrong and therefore developes a unique view about oneself and one's activities. This helps him to remember that to a karma yogi all work is equally lofty. For him the right action is the path which helps in the attainment of the ultimate goal of life.

The third form of yoga is the yoga of intellect or the Jyan yoga. This form of yoga is considered to be most difficult among all the forms of yoga. This is because Jyan yoga demands a cognitive approach to life. A Jyan yogi strives to attain oneness with the Absolute through an intuitive realisation. A practitioner of Jyan yoga strives to gain true knowledge (vidya) while trying to transgress the knowledge attained through the sense organs (avidya).

On the superficial level jyan yoga may appear like intellectualisation – a form of defensive coping with the problems of life. But jyan yoga is much more than that. It is a consciously adopted mode of life with a view to develop supra cognitive capacities so that one can cognise whatever is beyond the sensory capacities. Once such a capacity is developed one can easily experience oneness with the 'absolute power'.

Jyan yoga requires first of all a complete knowledge about the worldly reality as well as about the higher reality so that one can differentiate between the two. Such knowledge can be acquired through reading of scriptures which contain timeless knowledge. Once knowledge is acquired the jyan yogi has to gradually develop a capacity to regulate life through discretion and not on the basis of emotions. Gradually, a jyan yogi is able to see the fruitlessness of worldly life and futility of one's possessions including one's ego and that death is not the end of life. Such a person is able to look at life with equanimity, i.e. without being perturbed by loss or gain or being affected by pleasure and pain. Such a state is defined as the highest form of existence because it implies a true acceptance of reality of one's atman and the falseness of every thing else. It acts as a safeguard against denial for it helps in accepting the reality of death.

When we look at coping with stress from the view point of jyan yoga, we find that it is an integrated system of coping strategies being gradually recognised in the modern stress psychology. The most important strategies for jyan yoga are equanimity and acceptance.

The other important strategy is 'attention focussing'. A jyan yogi has to constantly focus attention on the ultimate goal of life i.e. the attainment of moksha. Attention focussing implies that for an ordinary person conflicts and distractions act as stressors since they call for energy expenditure. On the other hand one who has decided to work for a single goal, his energies are directed in only one direction, therefore there is no stress for him. But this goal must be the long term goal i.e., attaining of moksha and self realisation.

Self realisation does not come in a magical way but is attained through a lengthy process of cognitive learning whereby every object and every experience is given a new meaning. This learning may be explained as 'cognitive redefinition' wherein the objects and situations which arouse worldly desires are defined as redundant and those which repulse as non-personal. The task is difficult but a constant awareness of the ultimate goal frees a man from attachment with all objects till it becomes a way of life.

Like all learnings the task of knowing the path to 'moksha' is made easy when one gets help from a 'Guru'. Help is required because the path to moksha is not describable in words. It is through constant contact and getting subtle reinforcements that one is able to progress on this difficult path. Hence finding a genuine guru or a mentor becomes an important task for any individual who follows the path of jyan yoga. With constant support from one's guru or mentor one is able to carry on the meditational practice.

Anyone traversing the path of jyan yoga must overcome temptation of lust, pain or anger. Achievement of mastery over these forces provides secondary reinforcements so that one is able to become a 'sage of wisdom' a condition that provides a ground for the practice of meditation. By working hard for the attainment of the ultimate goal, slowly and slowly insight is developed till one is able to experience oneness with 'Brahaman'.

A form of yoga not so well known, in the stress field is Bhakti yoga or the yoga of devotion. This form of yoga can be described as a positive emotional attachment to one's personal God or to one's mentor. Any one who follows the path of Bhakti yoga gets intoxicated with love to the extent that the yogi sees God in every object and everywhere and in every living and non-living thing. Through this love the person experiences a pure bliss and no argument or barrier of any sort can change his way. Bhakti yoga therefore reduces stress through completely removing the cognitive overload. For a bhakti yogi all worldly activities that he does are a means of attaining the ultimate goal hence there is no dukha. In Gita Lord Krishna tells Arjun in clear terms:

> Those who fixing their mind on me, worship me ever steadfast and endowed with supreme faith, they are the best in yoga.
>
> (Gita XII/2)

And Kabir Das also declared that the study of innumerable books cannot provide the wisdom, while learning the true meaning of love (through experiencing it) brings total self-realisation.

In summary it can be said that according to Indian view, life itself is equivalent to stress as it involves separation from the 'origin'. Dutiful adoption of one's 'dharma' and ultimately following a path of yoga one can move away from the kleshas and the dukha and towards the ultimate goal of 'moksha', the eternal bliss. Examples abound in books and in common observation that the three paths of yoga converge towards the common goal. It is enough to give the examples of Vivekananda a Jyan yogi, Surdas and Mira as Bhakti yogi and Gandhi as Karma yogi.

Discussion

It is an accepted fact that the world images of a people play an important part in determining the meaning they give to their experiences. Most importantly the impact these experiences have on an individual is sanctioned by their world view.

In the formulation of this world view both ontogenic and phylogenic past are fused with each other. Together they determine a people's identity as well as what events and situations will be a threat and therefore a source of stress for them. Because of this reason understanding of the world view of a people carries a special significance in understanding the nature of stressors and the modes of coping adopted by any group of people.

The Indian view combines dharma i.e. the law of present life (the extent to which life of dharma is chosen) with 'Karma' i.e. the net balance of one's good and bad deeds of all the previous lives in determining what causes stress in him. Together they determine if the goals anyone sets lead towards or away from the path of moksha. In the course of working for various goals, depending upon how well they have been chosen, one experiences varied degrees of stress. Stress is also experienced when a person with such a view comes in contact with other viewpoints and tries to maintain a separate identity. But such encounters with counter viewpoints also provide opportunities for self evaluation and insights. The greatest strength of Indian viewpoint is that it provides a structured view of life, its origin and its ultimate end. It teaches that the 'Power' from which we have originated is the greatest power and that one will always be the part of that power. This wisdom, once attained helps to cope with all the stressful situations with equanimity. Also, when one selflessly follows the 'dharma' of one's stage of life and the designated role in society, step-by-step one moves towards Moksha and in transition experiences eternal bliss. In the words of Swami Vivekananda:

> Here is the world, and it is full of misery,
> Go out into it as Budha did, and struggle to
> lessen it or die in the attempt. Forget
> yourselves; this is the first lesson to be
> learnt, whether you are a theist or an atheist,
> whether you are an agnostic or a vedantist, a
> Christian or Muslim. The one lesson obvious
> to all is the destruction of little self and
> the building of the real self.

BIBLIOGRAPHY

Alexander, T., *Human Development in an Urban Age.* Engelwood Cliffs, NJ: Prentice Hall, Inc., 1973

Antonovsky, A., *Health, Stress and Coping: New Perspectives on Mental and Physical Well-being.* San Fransisco, CA: Jossey-Bass, 1979.

Appley, M.H. and Trumbull, R., Social Support as a Moderator of Life Stress, *Psychosomatic Medicine*, 1986 38, 300–314

Appley, M.H. and Trumbull, R., *Dynamics of Stress, Physiological Psychological and Social Perspectives.* New York: Plenum, 1986.

Averill, J.R., Personal control Over Aversive Stimuli and its Relationship to Stress. *Psychological Bulletin*, 1973, 80, 286–303.

Bandura, A., *Social Learning Theory.* Engelwood Cliffs. NJ: Prentice Hall, 1977.

Baum, A. and Valins, S., *Architecture and Social Behaviour: Psychological Studies of Social Density.* Hillside, NJ: Erlbaum, 1977.

Brady, J.V., Ulcers in Executive Monkeys. *Scientific American*, 1958, 199, 95–100.

Beck, A.T., *Coginitive Therapy and Emotional Disorders.* New York: International Universities Press, 1976.

Beech, H.R. and Vaughan, M., *A Behavioural Approach to the Management of Stress: A Practical Guide to Techniques.* Chichester, New York: Wiley, 1982.

Bhikkhu Khantipalo, *A Description of Dukkha. In the Basic Facts of Existence* Kandy: Buddhist Publication Society, 1981.

Benson, J.S. and Kennelly, K.J., Learned Helplessness: The result of Uncontrollable Aversive Stimuli?, *Journal of Personality and Social Psychology*, 1976, 34, 138–145.

Berkman, L.F. and Syme, S.L., Social Networks, Host Resistance and Mortality: A Nine-Year Follow Up Study of Alameda Country Residents. *American Journal of Epidemiology*, 1979, 109, 186–204.

Bernard, C., *Lecons sur les Proprietes Physiologiques et les Alterations Pathologiques des Liquids de L'organisme.* Vols. I and II, Paris: Balliere, 1859.

Birk, L., (Ed.), *Biofeedback*: Behavioural Medicine. New York: Grune and Stratton, 1973.

Brown, C.C., *Methods in Psychophysiology*. Baltimore, Md: William and Wilkins Co., 1967.

Brown G.W. and Andrews, B., Social Support and Depression: M.H Trumbul, *Dynamics of Stress*. New York: Plenum Press, 1986.

Byrne, D., Repression-Sensitisation as a Dimension of Personality. In B. Myer (Ed.), *Progress in Experimental Personality Research*, Vol. I. New York: Academic Press, 1983.

Burish, T.G. and Bradley, L.-A., (Eds.), *Coping with Chronic Disease: Research Applications*. New York: Academic Press, 1983.

Cannon, W.B., *Bodily Changes in Pain, Hunger, Fear and Rage*. New York: Appleton, 1929.

Cleary, A., Instrumentation for Psychology. Chichester: John Wiley & Sons, 1977.

Cobb, S., Social Support as a Moderator of Life Stress, *Psychosomatic Medicine*, 1976, 38, 300–314.

Cohen, S., Ewans, G., Stokols, D. and Krantz, D.S., *Behaviour, Health and Environmental Stress*. New York: Plenum, 1986.

Cohen, E.A., *Human Behaviour in Concentration Camps*. New York: Norton, 1953.

Cohen, S., After-effects of stress on Human Performance and Social Behaviour: A review of Research and Theory, *Psychological Bulletin*, 1980, 88, 82–108.

Coleman, V., *Stress Management Techniques*. Bombay: I.B.H., 1992.

Cousins. N., *Anatomy of an Illness: as Perceived by the Patient*. New York: Bantam Books, 1979.

Erickson, E., *Childhood and Society*. New York: W.W. Norton, 1963.

Everly, G.S. Jr, Rosenfeld, R. *The Nature and Treatment of the Stress Response: A Practical Guide for Clinicians*. 1981, New York: Plenum Press.

Frankenhaeuser, M., Psychoneuroendocrine Approaches to the Study of Emotion as Related to Stress and Coping. In H.W. Howe and R. Dienstbier, (Eds.), *Nebraska Symposium on Motivation, 1978*. Lincoln: University of Nebraska Press, 1979.

Gatchel, R.J., Baum, A. and Krantz, D.S., *An Introduction to Health Psychology*. New York: McGrawHill, 1989.

Gatchel, R.J. and Price, K.P., *Clinical Applications of Biofeedback: Appraisal and Status*. Elmsford, New York: Purgamon Press, 1979.

Glass, D.C. and Singer, J.E., Perceived Control of Aversive Stimulation and Reduction of Stress Responses. *Journal of Personality*, 1973, 101, 255–261.

Holmes, T.H. and Rahe. R.H., The Social Readjustment Rating Scale. *Journal of Psychosomatic Research*, 1967, 11, 213–218.

Humphreys, C., *Budhism: An Introduction and Guide*, London: Penguin Books, 1962.

Jacobs, H., *Western Psychotherapy and Hindu Sadhana*. London, George Allen and Unwin Ltd., 1961.

Jacobson, E., *Progressive Muscular Relaxation*. Chicago: University of chicago Press, 1938.

Jagannathan S., Hinduisms An Introduction, Bombay: Vakil, Feffer and Simons Ltd., 1989.

Janis, I.L., *Psychological Stress: Psychoanalytical and Behavioural Studies of Surgical Patients*. New York: Praeger Press, 1982.

Janis, I.L. *Stress Attitudes and Decisions*. New York: Praeger Press, 1982.

Jenkins, C.D., Recent Evidence Supporting Psychologic and Social Risk Factor for Coronary Disease. *New England Journal of Medicine*, 1976, 294, 987–994, 1033–1038.

Johnson, J.E., Stress Reduction Through Sensation Information In I.D. Sarason and C.D. Spielberger (Eds.), *Stress and Anxiety*, Vol. 2, Washington, D.C.: Hemisphere, 1975.

Kanner, A.D., Coyne, J.C., Schaeffer, C. and Lazarus R.S., Comparison of two Modes of Stress Measurement: Daily Hassles and Uplifts Versus Major Life Events. *Journal of Behavioural Medicine*, 1981, 4, 1–39.

Kakkar, S., *The Inner World: A Psychoanalytic study of Childhood and Society in India*. Delhi: Oxford University Press, 1982.

Kasl, S.V. and Cooper, C.L.(Eds.), *Stress and Health: Issues in Research Methodology*, John Wiley & Sons Ltd., 1987.

Khorana, S.A., Psychological Risk Factors in Ischaemic Heart Disease. *Indian Journal of Clinical Psychology*, 1989, 16, 13–17.

Kobasa S.C., Stressful Life Events, Personality and Health: An Inquiry Into Hardiness. *Journal of Personality and Social Psychology*, 1979, 37, 1-11.

Lazarus, R.S. and Folkman, S., *Stress Appraisal and Coping*. New York: Springer, 1984.

Lazarus, R.S., *Psychological Stress and Coping Process*. New York: McGraw-Hill, 1966.

Lefcourt, H.M., Repression Sensitisation: A measure of the Evaluation of Emotional Expression. *Journal of Consulting Psychology*. 1966, 30, 444–449.

Levi, L., *Preventing Work Stress*. Reading, MA: Addison-Wesley, 1981.

Levine S. and Ursin H., (Eds.), *Coping and Health*. New York: Plenum Press, 1979.

Locke, S.E, Hurst, M.W., Heisel, J.S., Kraus, L. and Williams, R.M., The Influences of Stress and Other Psychological Factors on Human Immunity. Paper presented at the American Psychosomatic Society Meeting, Boston, 1979.

Luczak, H., The use of stimulators in testing individual working capacity. Ergonomics, 1971, 14, 651–660.

Matarazzo, J.D., Behavioural Immunogens and Pathogens in Health and Illness. In B.L. Hamonds and C.J. Scheirer (Eds.), Psychology and Health: The Master Lecture Series, Vol. 3, Washington D.C.: American Psychological Association, 1984.

Miechenbaum, D.H., *Cognitive-behaviour Modification*. New York: Plenum. 1977.

Nagendra, H.R. and Nagarathna, R., *New Perspectives in Stress Management*. Bangalore: Vivekand Kendra, 1988.

Palsane, M.N., Bhavasar, S.N., Goswami, R.P. and Evans, G.W., *The Concept of Stress in Indian Tradition*. Publication No. 5, School of Behavioural Science, Pune: University of Poona, 1993.

Pervin, L.A., The need to Predict and Control Under Conditions of Threat, *Journal of Personality*, 1963, 31, 570–587.

Pestonjee, D.M., *Stress and Coping*. New Delhi: Sage Publishers, 1982.

Rabkin, J.G., and Struening, E.L., Life Events, Stress and Illness. *Science*, 1976, 191, 1013–1020.

Rao, K., Subbakrishna, D.K. and Prabhu, G.G., Development of a Copying Checklist: A Preliminary Report. *Indian Journal of Psychiatry*, 1989, 31, 128–133.

Roskies, E. and Lazarus, R.S., *Coping Life Styles*. New York: Bruner/Mazel, 1980.

Satyanand, D. Dynamic Psychology of the Gita of Hinduism. Delhi: Oxford & IBH Publishing Co., 1972.

Schmale, A.H., Jr., Giving-up as a Final Pathway to Changes in Health. *Advances in Psychosomatic Medicine*, 1972, 8, 20–40.

Schulz, R., Effects of Control and Predictability on the Physical and Psychological Well-being of the Institutionalized Aged. *Journal of Personality and Social Psychology*, 1976, 33, 563–573.

Seligman, M.E.P., *Helplessness: On depression, Development and Death*. San Fransisco: W.H. Freeman, 1975.

Selye, H., *The Stress of Life*. New York: McGraw-Hill, 1976.

Selye, H.(Ed.), *Selye's Guide to Stress Research*, Vol. I. New York: Van Nostrand Reinhold, 1980.

Sidowski, J.B., (Ed.), *Experimental Methods and Instrumentation in Psychology*. New York: McGrawHill, 1966.

Sinha, J., *Indian Psychology*, Vol. I, Delhi: Motilal Banarsi Das, 1985.

Sinyor, D., Schwarts, J.G., Peronnet, F., Bisson, G., and Seraganian, P., Aerobic Fitness Level and Reactivity to

Psychosocial Stress. *Psychosomatic Medicine*, 1983, 45, 205–217.

Srivastava, S. *Stress Personality and Cancer*. New Delhi: National Book Organisation, 1988.

Srivastava, S., Coping Styles and Cancer Incidents. *DEI Research, Journal of Education and Psychology*, 1990, 29–34.

Stein, M., Keller, S.E. and Scheifer, S.J., Stress and Immunomodulation: The Role of Depression and Neuroendocrine Function. *Journal of Immunology*, 1985, 135, (2) (suppl.), 827–833.

Syme, S.L., Life Style Intervention in Choice-Based Trials, *American Journal of Epidemiology*, 1978, 108, 87–91.

The Holy Gita, Commentary by Swami Chinmayananda, Bombay: Central Chinmaya Mission Trust.

Turk, D.C., Meichenbaum, D.H. and Berman, W.H., Application of Biofeedback for the Regulation of Pain: A Critical Review. *Psychological Bulletin*, 1979, 86, 1322–1338.

Wakhlu, K.L., and Wakhlu, O.N., *Kidnapped: 45 days with Militants in Kashmir*. Delhi: Konark Publishers, 1993.

Walster, E., Assignment of Responsibility for an Accident. *Journal of Personality and Social Psychology*, 1966, 3, (1), 73–79.

Wills, T.A., Supportive Functions of Interpersonal Relationships. In: S. Cohen and S.L. Syme (Eds.), Social Support and Health. Orlando, Fla: Academic Press, 1985.